Economic Insights:

Pluralist Arguments against Economic Orthodoxy.

Volume 2

Economic Insights:

Volume 2

Capital, Money, Distribution, Production, Labour & Wages, Power, Business, Policy, Misc.

by

Dr. Fred Day[1]

Praescientia Press

"For Science and for Art"

Contents

List of Insights

Economic Insights:

Pluralist Arguments against Economic Orthodoxy.

This work is volume 2 of our collection of economic ideas and insights formulated over recent years. Each represents an adventure against standard, i.e. superficial economic ideas, concepts and orthodoxy.

They are presented in roughly subject based sections, rather than a chronological order. Many are relatively short portions, although some are more developed over numerous pages. Some portions are the result of combining otherwise individual insights, whereas others are very specific and targeted.

As insights, they need to be recognized as often being in their formative rather than complete and complex state. Most would benefit from further research. Some will only attain full fruition by cross fertilization with other economic ideas and/or with inter-disciplinary concepts.

This work, being merely a collection of only vaguely connected insights, I tend to call *the Green Book*, simply because of its cover. Our *Volume 1* (the Yellow Book) contained the first four sections, Methodology, Paradigms, Process Economics, and Quantum Based Economics.

This second volume is made up of the remaining nine sections:

Subject Based Sections:-

5) Capital   6) Money

7) Distribution   8) Production

9) Labour & Wages   10) Power

11) Business   12) Policy

13) Misc.

Frédéric Bastiat pointed out that it is the un-foreseeable economic consequences of human action that are generally the most important aspects. The ability to recognise the least obvious outcomes and consequences is the most valuable skill that an economist can possess and should accordingly be developed.

This requires the cultivation of pluralist perspectives and a conscious awareness of the history of economic thought and ideas. A unified economic orthodoxy as a disciplined paradigm is counter-productive not only for a dynamic economy, but also to a creative Economics.

Following Bastiat, what distinguishes us as economists, are the views we take of the economy, and its relationship within the wider human society.

Given that we are here primarily unconcerned with presenting new paradigmatic economic discoveries or inventions, what we can and should present are our views, perspectives, and interpretations of the events, processes and manifestations within the economy.

We should be more artists, than scientists or technicians. These insights are the prime outputs of those Bastiat cited as good Economists. All else is vanity.

As educators, the economist's role is not only to communicate economic insights, but to inculcate the origination of such personal insights to our students. A degree in Economics should provide its holder with the indispensable skills to be similarly creative. These essential abilities will not only be a technical knowledge of various economic theories and ideas, but critical reasoning and evaluation skills.

Too much emphasis is often focused upon the technical, scientific, and mathematical aspects of what an economist is supposed to do, rather than the artistic qualities that furnish a prospective economist with what they are supposed to be.

When one looks in a concentrated and disciplined manner, all one is likely to see is what one is primarily looking at. Creativity is looking at something and seeing something more. It is having the imagination to see something new; something that does not yet exist, except in the mind's eye.

When one observes a multitude, rather than a singularity, the brain will select different combinations out from the various possibilities in its attempt to make sense of what is presented before it. Many of these attempts may be meaningless, or even misleading, but just a few may be valuable for the insights they provide. What appears as creativity, may simply be unconscious attempts at cognitive comprehension.

The insights here, are, at times, intentionally personal and sometimes casual, we make no apology for this. Hopefully its reader will gain an understanding of why this is, as they progress through these insights. However, it must be admitted that we are reminded by Henry Hetherington that:

As life is uncertain, it behoves everyone to make preparations for death. I deem it therefore a duty incumbent on me, ere I quit this life, to express in writing, for the satisfaction and guidance of esteemed friends, my feelings and opinions in reference to our common principles (Hetherington, 1849, p.237).

Volume 2:- Section 5
Capital

Insight 71:
Notes on Polymodalism

How can capital be other than polymodal, when its constituents are heterogeneous? Even a single incident of Capital can be heterogeneous from one moment to the next. This is not the simple heterogeneousness of Capital goods, i.e. *typewriters* compared to *lawnmowers,* but rather the heterogeneity of *Capital goods* to *Financial Capital* to *Human Capital* to *Intellectual Capital* to *Capital as Power* to *Capital as a Process*.

Polymodal Capital
Capital is polymodal in that it is multifaceted and necessarily exists in numerous modes, states and conditions. It is not a single entity but *schizophrenic* (or schizoid). A *21st Century Schizoid Capital*. Indeed, all the factors of production - Capital, Labour and Land are polymodal in that they are not single entities.

Some revenues, such as income from inherited capital should be seen as rent. So, the apparent rent generating capital can be considered as both Capital and/or Land (as in Nassau Senior). Further complications can arise when Labour is seen as a form of Capital (as, for example, in Edward Kellogg's *Labor and Other Capital* [1849]).

Entrepreneurship is now often used as a fourth factor of production. Whereas others also use such entities as Natural Resources as an additional Factor.

In the book *Intequisms: Accounting of Ideas* [Pienaar, M.D. (2014)], the neologism "intequity"[2], is used as a term to describe an entity abstracted from equity to create a new production factor within capitalism. Equity, when regarded as part of capital, is divided into equity and intequity. Entrepreneurship is divided into network related matters and other created related matters. Network related matters function in the sphere of equity; whereas the other created related matters reside in the spheres of intequities.

Economic activity is by its very makeup and constituents, polymodal. There are no applicable definitions for economic terms, just as there are, to use an evolutionary analogy from Alfred Wallace, no species, but only individualised instances or moments. Although, as George Shackle (1964)[3] pointed out, human nature is such that we tend to allocate individuals to pigeonholes and thereby stereotype them. Definitions appear to be necessities within human thought schemes.

Materialism and Idealism
There is a link between materialism and the drive to classify all events so as to define, and thereby measure,

---

[2] The term intequity can also be found used to signify international equity as opposed to domestic equity (domequity). As in the paper *Mountain or Molehill? The pervasiveness of overstated earnings through the expected rate of return on defined benefit pension plan assets*. (Brian Adams, Mary Margaret Frank and Tod Perry August 2008). https://papers.ssrn.com/sol3/papers.cfm?abstract_id=1408215
[3] *General Thought-Schemes and the Economist: Woolwich Economic Lecture*, 1964.

all individuals. Does an Idealistic perspective, without an exclusively material notion of reality, provide a more workable, realistic, or true conceptualisation of reality?

Are we saying that economic elements suffer non-specificity? Is that just an unrelated statistical term, given that specificity does have a particular meaning? Are we saying that our economic elements are prone to too high an incident of both false positives and false negatives? Is this relevant? Or do these terms quantify the measure of our definitional errors? Would this be relevant or of any theoretical or practical purposes?

By non-specificity we mean having the character of not being definable or otherwise subject to specification. As distinguished from the technical statistical term specificity. Most of the technical terms in economics are subject to non-specificity.

There is an idea that everything that exists can be specified and thereby quantified. This is usually referred to as the scientific method. This thereby excludes any reference to or acknowledgment of ideas or any other non-specifiable element.

It is somewhat ironic that this scientific idea itself cannot itself exist, and presumably therefore does not exist. Ideas cannot be measured. Unfortunately, for economics, as Nassau Senior highlighted, its constituents are predominantly mental concepts and thereby unmeasurable; presumably thereby have no substantial existence.

All the technical terms, therefore, of Political Economy, represent either purely mental ideas, such as *demand*, *utility*, *value*, and *abstinence*, or objects, which, though some of them may be material, are considered by the political economist so far only as they are the results or causes of certain affections of the human mind, such as *wealth, capital, rent, wages,* and *profits*. (Senior, 1854, p.35)

Contextualisation

The definition of Capital, for example, is contextual. The same thing will essentially change its very nature according to the contexts in which it is viewed, used, conceived, owned and combined with other constituents. The natures of material elements are contextually dependent upon the ideas with which they are mingled and understood.

Money illusion is a crucial issue within economics, but it, like the bulk of what is actually important therein, is unquantifiable and therefore unmeasurable. The importance of these otherwise intangible idea concepts does not go unrecognised. We can see this, for example, in things like business confidence and sentiment surveys, where completely immeasurable ideas are subject to bogus quantitative measurements.

An interesting point from these surveyed or indexed measures is the effective admission that these so-called quantities cannot be done with cardinality. We can survey business confidence, but all we can really say is that it is either higher, lower or unchanged comparatively, than some previous level.

This ordinal ranking is to be found in other measures. For example, temperature scales are actually ordinal, although presented as cardinal. 20 degrees Celsius is not twice as hot as 10 degrees, as 68 degrees Fahrenheit is not twice as hot as 50 degrees in the alternative scale. All that these respective scales tell us is ordinarily. This necessarily also applies to any other indexed scale.

Thus, it is a misnomer to claim that inflation has doubled if the CPI figure goes up from 1% to 2%. To be accurate, all that can be said is that the CPI figure has doubled. This likewise applies to other so called important data such as stock price indexes.

This could be said of much of other data, such as money prices, particularly in real terms. As such, most of the data utilised in economics are only pseudo figures that at best only provide rankings or ordinality, rather than cardinal quantification. Admittedly, this tends to be partly recognized with the most crucial measure in economics, i.e. value.

The temperature allusion illustrates an inherent problem with quantification in that the choice of scale is a concept or idea and not necessarily a material quantum. Indeed, the idea of money as expressed in the multitude of national currencies is a prime example of this relativity within economics. This is especially true when ideas such as Capital or value are expressed (albeit for convenience) in a nominal currency form. The selection of a standard nominal or universal currency, such as the dollar, illustrates the transient and arbitrary nature of many quantitative units.

Insight 72:
Capital and the *Naïve Productivity* Principle

Within an equitable or meritocratic scheme of distributive justice the rewards, outcomes or *Product* of society's production should be allocated proportionally to the productivity of the contributing factors; *Land*, Labour and *Capital*.

However we are faced with the problem that in reality it seems otherwise. In modern capitalistic production the rewards of production are apparently distributed according to the apparent power (i.e. their importance or bargaining power) of the participants. Thus, they are not allocated according to the relative productivity of the contributing factors. As such, power seeking participants will necessarily be motivated to seek an increase in their power, so as to increase their reward (i.e. profit).

This leads to a gate-keeper problem, in that arbitrary power, in the guise of *Capital*, is sought rather than productivity. In this way Capital has assumed a mantle of prominence and superiority that is not otherwise warranted. Capital's economic dominance within Capitalism is due to assumed significance rather than any actual productivity.[4]

When one ponders why Capital's productive worth is almost universally accepted one might perhaps see an

---

[4] Although the name Capital, when defined as that which is most important, as in the supporting head of a column, seems to be evidence of the long establish acknowledgement and understanding of this point.

answer in Behavioural Economics.[5] Behavioural biases (for example, Dispositional Effects, Anchoring and Endowment Biases) are such that unwarranted value is attached solely from long established practice.

This notion of *Naïve Productivity*, identified by Böhm-Bawerk, can be associated with economic sabotage, whereby lower productivity is sought as a means to increasing power, and hence profits.

For a system of distribution to be equitable it should be based on the productiveness of the contributors not simply the relative power of the participants.[6]

---

[5] We will elsewhere be drawn into considerations of principal–agent problems in relation to these issues as it appears that power of agents now has sovereignty over the productiveness of the principals.

[6] This, effectively, can be seen explored in the work of David Ellerman with his discussions of jurisprudence and the nature of the firm.

Insight 73:
Capital as Business

If Capital is a Process, is that Process what is usually denominated Business?[7]

If Capital is power and thereby a process: and Business is "the realm of power"[8]: does this mean that capital is Business?

Therefore, to paraphrase Hodgskin:-

"In fact business seems to mean, when ultimately analysed, little more than, or be very little different from, the power of one man, however obtained, over the labour or produce of the labour of another."[9]

---

[7] See Volume 1 Insight 54: *Towards a view of Capital as a Process.*

[8] "the realm of power that, in the capitalist epoch, takes the form of business" (*Capital as power: Toward a new cosmology of capitalism* Shimshon Bichler and Jonathan Nitzan, *Real-World Economics Review,* issue no. 61, 2012, page 77)

[9] Original in *The Economist* (Hodgskin, 30th Dec. 1854, p.1454)

Insight 74:
Towards a View
of Capital as *Business:*

Introduction

These notes intend to investigate the concept that Capital can be seen not simply as a social relation but as having the character of a series of processes. Consequentially it should be understood as being consubstantial with business. In order to achieve this perspective, we need to look at the historical development of concerns with the nature of Capital; starting with Charles Hall and other classical economists and concluding with the position of the Capital as Power (CasP) Forum.

We thereby aim to be able to meld two otherwise separate concepts within Bichler and Nitzan's *Capital as Power* Forum – the antagonism between business and Industry with the concept of Capital as a power relationship.

The Notion of Capital

No term in economical language has been used in so many different senses as the word Capital: and there is no subject in the whole range of the science of Political Economy on which eminent writers have differed so widely. (Senior, 1848, p.310)

For Classical Economists their fundamental questions resolved around topics concerned with the nature of the elemental constituents within their discipline. They were thus troubled with issues such as Prices, and the three factors of production; Land, Labour and Capital. There were questions regarding Value that have subsequently often been interpreted within a Labour Theory of Value perspective, but these were subsidiary to their main categorical enquiries.

The new science of Political Economy had to establish its credibility by solidifying not only its terms of reference but also, at least initially, simply the nomenclature it used. Therefore, each economist had to clarify what they meant by the various formulations of Price (such as Normal, Nature, Real, Money, Social, etc.), as well as what might appear more concrete terms such as Labour and Capital.

Hence, there were ideas that encompassed Labour or was alternatively a specific form of Labour, as an expression of Capital. As, for example, in Edward Kellogg's *Labor and Other Capital* (1849).

Capital and Land
There were also discussions over whether Land was a peculiar variety of Capital. For example, Nassau Senior aligned Capital and Land within his discussion of the difficulties in differentiating rent from profits:

> the distinction of profit from rent ceases as soon as the capital, from which a given revenue arises, has become, whether by gift or by inheritance, the property of a person to whose abstinence and exertions it did not owe its creation. The revenue arising from a dock, or a wharf, or a canal, is profit in the hands of the *original constructor*. It is the reward of *his* abstinence in having employing capital for the purposes of production instead of for those of enjoyment. But in the hands of his heir it has all the attributes of rent. It is to him the gift of

fortune, not of a sacrifice. It may be said, indeed, that such a revenue is the reward for the owner's abstinence in not selling the dock or canal and spending its price in enjoyment. But the same remark applies to every species of transferable property. Every estate may be sold, and the purchase money wasted. If the last basis of classification were adopted, the greater part of what every Political Economist has termed rent must be called profit. (Senior, 1836, p.129)

Senior seems to have accepted that inherited capital (unearned or *appropriated capital*) could be deemed to be receiving rent, not profit. If we accept Ricardo's proposition that all rent was a transfer of wealth away from the productive agents, then we arrive at an understanding akin to Hodgskin's, whereby income derived from this particular form of capital is, as Lord Lauderdale (James Maitland), feared, designated as unproductive and to be a derivative of the wealth created by active agents of production transferred to idle capitalists.

Senior did not pursue this analysis further but preferred to return to the established conception accepting its imprecision in favour of convenience.

In this, however, as in many other cases, the inconveniences occasioned by a departure from an established nomenclature and an established classification are so great, that we do not think that they will be compensated by the nearer approach to precision. (Senior, 1836, p.133)

George Poulett Scrope had likewise discussed the identity of capital, land and labour and resolved that this was "over-refining" pursued in order to give "accuracy to definitions and propositions" but were thereby impractical and unworkable (Scrope, 1833, p.142*n*)

> If such definitions are adopted, Political Economy becomes at once an entire jumble of meaningless phrases: land, labour, and capital, – rent, wages, and profits, are all different words for the same thing; – production and consumption are indistinguishable; "And nought is everything, and everything is nought." (ibid, p.143*n*)[10]

Overall these concerns with the factors of production were not unrelated to the practical necessity of analysing economic growth and development. This was particularly evident at this period when the Industrial Revolution had forced its way into everyone's attention. If economics was expected to come to any practical understanding of reality it was seen that a comprehension of industrialised production was one question it could cut its intellectual teeth upon.

Differing Emphasises

One can view the Marginalist Revolution as a change of emphasis, within an Aristotelian causality perspective, from a concentration with Efficient Causes to a focus on Final Causes. Thus J.S. Mill and other humanistic economists saw Economics as primary concerned with Labour and its results, whereas later post-1880s economists increasingly directed their attention to

---

[10] "Thinking is but an idle waste of thought, And nought is everything, and everything is nought." Was an oft quoted comment by the English poet Horace Smith (1777-1849). It stems from a work Smith published with his brother James Smith;- *Rejected Addresses: Or, The New Theatrum Poetarum* (1812).

consumers' subjective marginalist decision making processes.

Indeed, it could be argued that the Classical Economists, whilst attempting to conceive of their science as a natural science, saw entities such as Prices, Land, Labour and Capital, even if they could not collectively formalise their definitions, as permanent fixed unchanging categories.

The change of scientific viewpoint during the nineteenth century that saw Nature, as a physical reality, transformed from one of solid permanency to a universe of constant and inevitable flux (e.g. evolution). As such economists could no longer conceive these economic categories as fixed elements capable of finite definition. The conceptions of process, change and development became central themes and fundamental categories of science in general as well as economics in particular.

Despite this refocusing of attention, Capital as the hub of Capitalistic production still tended to be viewed as a concrete element definable in what might be seen as Classical terms, even within modern Neo-Classical economics.[11]

Notwithstanding, or perhaps because of, Marx's attempts at quantifying Capital, and partly because they forget (or are ignorant of) the outcome of the subsequent Cambridge Capital Controversy, many of today's economists can be seen to have only a sketchy grasp on the nature of Capital. Indeed, this lack of an adequate grip on the subject should perhaps be seen as not

---

[11] *Capitalism Without Capital: The Rise of the Intangible Economy* by Jonathan Haskel and Stian Westlake (2017) provides a useful example of an exception to the preoccupation with the concrete.

unconnected with mainstream economists' inability to have accurately foreseen the inevitability and the scale of recent financial disasters that have beset *capital markets* and the *economy* in general.

Some economists, such as the Austrian School, have long warned of the orthodoxy's lack of understanding of the reality of Capital. There are also more modern attempts being made to understand Capital in qualitative rather than exclusively quantitative terms, such as Bichler and Nitzan.

Thus, research to comprehend Capital is productive on several levels. A dialogue with heterodox and pluralist economic perspectives will be invaluable in formulating a position with merit in what are undoubtedly controversial areas. These various areas of research are all closely knit and thereby inter-related. As a research project they should bear fruit when meshed together as a whole rather than scattered as individual and isolated fragments.

In a spirit of contextualising current Political Economists' efforts to comprehend Capital it would be well to give a historical overview of economists who have highlighted some of the problems with Capital.

Problems with Capital:
Identification of the structural issues with Capital can be seen to begin with the discussion of Wealth within the work of Charles Hall (1740–1825) in his *The Effects of Civilization* (1805):

> The possession, therefore, of those things which can obtain and command the labour of man, is to be considered as wealth. Wealth, therefore, is the possession of that which gives power over, and commands the labour of man: it is,

therefore, power; and into that, and that only, ultimately resolvable. (Hall, 1805, p.48)

Hall's insights were later developed by Percy Ravenstone (an anonymous pseudonym) in his/her two works: *A Few Doubts as to the Correctness of the Opinions generally maintained on the Subjects of Population and Political Economy* (1821) and *Thoughts on the Funding System and its Effects* (1824).[12]

A Few Doubts was a scathing critique of Malthusian economics, that adopted a strictly Lockean standpoint whereby the natural right to private property is the right to the work of one's own hands. Edward Seligman summarised that Ravenstone's stance identified property rights as the fundamental issue:

> Property alone confers power, its rights are considered more sacred than those of industry, and the interests of the poor are sacrificed to those of the rich. (Seligman, 1903)

Seligman thus recognised Ravenstone's concerns that the rights of endowed property supplanted those of labourers (*industry* in the parlance of the early 19th century). For Ravenstone another fundamental issue was the ethereal nature of Capital:

> It is not a very easy matter, however, to acquire an accurate idea of the nature of capital. It is quite another sort of being from its confederates. … It has none but a metaphysical existence.

---

[12] Both Hall and Ravenstone are classed as a Ricardian Socialists even though Hall's work was published before Ricardo had published any work. It can also be noted that Thomas Hodgskin is often similarly classified, even though he was opposed both to Ricardo's economics and to socialism.

Though its effects be everywhere felt, its presence can nowhere be detected. ... Its incorporeal nature for ever eludes our grasp. No man hath seen its form; none can tell its habitation. Its power resides not within itself, it never acts but by borrowed means. They may be increased to any imaginable amount without adding to the real riches of a nation. ... Capital is like the subtle ether of the older philosophers; it is around us, it about us, it mixes in everything we do. Though itself invisible, its effects are but too apparent. It is no less useful to our œconomists than that was to the philosophers. It serves to account for whatever cannot be accounted for in any other way." (Ravenstone, 1821, p.293)

A Barrier to Production:

The last chapter of Hodgskin's *Popular Political Economy* (1827) was entitled *Effects of the Accumulation of Capital*. It was here that he most vividly expressed the negative effect of capital accumulation upon production

> though every portion of capital brings a profit *to its owner*, it depends on the nature of the capital itself, whether it assist production. But a great quantity of capital is always lent to share the revenue or produce of others, and this portion can have no beneficial effect on the wealth of the whole. What enriches the individual capitalist does not necessarily add to national wealth. (Hodgskin, 1827, p.243: *CW*, Vol. VI, p.203)

In so far as capital embodied previous labour brought to bear, it was a boon to production. Whereas when capital embodied the socially unproductive activities of idle capitalists, it was a hindrance and drain upon production.

In response to Hodgskin, Capital ceased to be exclusively thought of as a stock, but was increasing recognised as a flow; paving the way for the eventual recantation of the Wage Fund theory. New theoretical justifications for capital divorced from productivity, mainly concerned with abstinence, increasingly saw profits as the reward for the capitalists' sacrifice and saving.

Karl Marx identified [in his *Theories of Surplus Value* part 1 (1863)] the main proposition of *Labour Defended* :

> it bursts forth with the general statement, which is the inevitable consequence of Ricardo's presentation – that *capital is unproductive*. (Marx, 1863, p.266)

For Marx, Hodgskin was one of the first to recognise that capital was more than just physical entities, but amounted to a social relationship.

> The economists do not conceive of capital as a relation. They cannot do so without at the same time conceiving it as a historically transitory, i.e., a relative – not an absolute – form of production. Hodgskin himself does not share this concept. Insofar as it justifies capital it does not justify its justification by the economist, but on the contrary refutes it. (ibid, p.274)

Indeed, in *Labour Defended* (1825) Hodgskin had also identified a central feature of the Cambridge Capital Controversies – the inherent difficulty of quantifying Capital:

it is not, however, the quantity but the quality of the fixed capital on which the productive industry of a country depends. Instruments are productive, to use the improper language of the Political Economist, not in proportion as they multiplied, but as they are efficient. (Hodgskin, 1825, p.19: *CW*, Vol. I, p.39)

Hodgskin went on to emphasise that "the quantity of commodities they produce will depend on the efficiency of their fixed capital" (ibid, p.20). However, "quantity" was misprinted as "quality" in the 1922 edition. This was a crucial error given that Hodgskin was writing about the distinction between "quantity" and "quality" in terms of capital's efficiency. The phrase "the quality of commodities they produce will depend on the efficiency of their fixed capital" (as in the 1922 edition) is less significant than Hodgskin's original words: "the quantity of commodities they produce will depend on the efficiency of their fixed capital", as this is a far more consequential statement.

Hodgskin was originally stressing that the quantity of output does not bare a direct relationship to the simple quantity of capital, but that it was the quality of capital (i.e. the current level of technical, social and cultural knowledge) that was the critical factor in determining levels of output.

Thus Hodgskin's emphasise was lost in the 1922 edition. Unfortunately, it is this 1922 edition that has become the basis of most of the subsequent printed and online versions of *Labour Defended*. Hodgskin later published an updated edition in 1831, however this edition is rarely available and seldom referred to.

Naïve Productivity Theory

Hodgskin's attack on Capital as a hindrance to production amounts to a condemnation of what was subsequently identified by Eugen von Böhm-Bawerk as the Naïve Productivity Theory.

> Those productivity theories which claim for capital a direct value-producing power (first type), as well as those which start from the physical productivity of capital, but believe that the phenomenon of surplus value is self-evidently and necessarily bound up with it (second type), ... I shall group these together under name of Naïve Productivity theories. (Böhm-Bawerk, 1890, p.118-9)

These theories thus maintained that capital was actively productive of value or wealth.

Although Böhm-Bawerk assigned J.B. Say as "The founder of the Naïve Productivity theories" (ibid, p.120), this concept was also raised by James Maitland (Lord Lauderdale) in his *An Inquiry into the Nature and origin of Public Wealth* (1804):

> By what means Capital or stock contributes to wealth is not so apparent. What is the nature of the profit of stock? and how does it originate? are questions the answers to which do not immediately suggest themselves. (Maitland, 1804, p.155)

Maitland (and Say) placed the productivity of capital at the crux of the issue of the rewards to capital. Maitland had started by referring to the writings of one of the prime inspirations for Hodgskin – John Locke – who had envisaged profits as the product of labour that were not actively caused by the productivity of capital. Maitland cited the following passage from Locke's *Some Considerations of the Consequence of lowering Interest and raising the Value of Money* (1692 edition): -

> but money is a barren thing and produces nothing; but by compact transfers that profit that was the reward of one man's labour into another man's pocket. (Locke, 1692, p.53 [cited in Maitland, 1804, p.157])

This was evidently an unsettling notion for the Lord Lauderdale or any other *Idle Capitalist*:

> If this, however, was a just and accurate idea of the profit of capital, it would follow that the profit of stock must be a derivative, not an original source of revenue; and capital could not therefore be considered as a source of wealth, its profits being only a transfer from the pocket of the labourer into that of the proprietor of stock. (Maitland, 1804, p.157-8)

This passage would be a good summary of what was to become Hodgskin's position – that capital was not productive and that profits and rents were sums extracted from the productivity of the labourers. To counter this argument Lauderdale tried to show that capital was of itself an active (productive) agent of production. Rather than delve deeply into Lauderdale's defence of capital we can use his conclusion which related to the productive services provided by capital and again expressed the notion of capital performing labour;

> Now, it is apprehended, that in every instance where capital is so employed as to produce a profit, it uniformly arises, either – *from supplanting a portion of labour, which would*

- 31 -

otherwise be performed by the hand of man; or
*– from its performing a portion of labour, which
is beyond the reach of the personal exertion of
man to accomplish.* (Maitland, 1804, p.161)

It was (in part) against this Naïve Productivity theory
as expressed by Maitland and Say that Hodgskin wrote
Labour Defended.

Modern Marginal Productivity theory still maintains
such a notion of productivity. However, if we understand
that marginal productivity should deliver capital its
appropriate profit in perfect competition, but note that the
theoretical rate of profit in perfect competition is zero,
then perhaps the Marginal Productivity of Capital can be
understood to be zero. If capital receives higher rates of
profit within imperfect competition, this must surely be
due to power relations rather than any inherent
profitability of capital?

Contrasting Industry to Business:
An interesting start to understanding Capital
conceptually as a process can be made in line with the
contemporary political economy of the *Capital as Power
Forum* which commences its conceptualisations with a
perspective based on Thorstein Veblen. This in turn can
be seen as, in essence, owing much to classical
economists such as Hodgskin and Ravenstone. They
(i.e. Bichler and Nitzan) investigate Capital and
interrogate the relationships between Business and
Industry.

A key to grasping this relationship is an understanding
of the term Industry from a Classical rather than modern
Neoclassical viewpoint. Industry is thereby the collective
activity of humans to improve their conditions. Such
improvements include the production of material goods

and services that add to overall social welfare and which can thereby be conceived of as wealth.

The everyday enrichment of life thus results from purposive human activities that were otherwise named as *Industry*. Indeed, although this term is now often associated with large scale or factory based activities, it was in the early 19th century used to simply differentiate productiveness from idleness. Industry was that which was industrious and in the main, that was labour.

> Industry, understood as the collective knowledge and creative effort of humanity, is inherently cooperative, integrated and synchronized. It operates best when its various events resonate with each other. (Bichler and Nitzan, 2012, p.77)[13]

It was thus that Veblen contrasted industry to business, so that the latter was distinctly less productive than the former. Indeed, business was for Veblen (and modern political economists such as Bichler and Nitzan) activity opposed to industry and its aim to improve the human condition. Hence his adoption of the term *Sabotage* to describe the principal mechanisms of business.

> Business, in contrast, is not collective; it is private. Its goals are achieved through the threat and exercise of systemic prevention and restriction – that is, through strategic sabotage. The key object of this sabotage is the resonating pulses of industry – a resonance that business

---

[13] *Capital as power: Toward a new cosmology of capitalism* Shimshon Bichler and Jonathan Nitzan, *Real-World Economics Review,* issue no. 61, 26th Sept. 2012, page 77 http://www.paecon.net/PAEReview/issue61/BichlerNitzan61.pdf

constantly upsets through built-in dissonance. (ibid)

Capital as Processes

Our understanding of Capital will be further enhanced with an understanding of the relationship betwixt Capital and business.

Hodgskin seemed to equate Capital with various processes of control over the workers:

> it is plain that capital, or the power to employ labour, and co-exiting labour are one; and, that productive capital and skilled labour are also one; consequently, capital and a labouring population are precisely synonymous (Hodgskin, 1825, p.33: *CW*, Vol. I, p.61)

This is Hodgskin's unclaimed acknowledgement that Capital amounted to various processes. Indeed, we can thereby conceive of Capital as an accumulation of social and individual processes. The idea of Capital as processes is thus commensurate with its immeasurability. Capital is a succession of evolving conglomerations of processes that generally carries the title:- Business.

Capital, as the exercise of power, when formalised, requires a series of processes. Business likewise, as a series of formalised processes, amounts to the exercise of power. As such both business and Capital are specifically the exercise of power within the field of production (in a generalized form). Thereby there is much that aligns the two concepts. So much so that they might, with much fairness be seen as equivalent. Capital can thus be conceived as business.

Essentially what is meant by this is that Capital, business, and the power over Labour are consubstantial. This is particularly the case within a modern economy dominated by the ideologies of Neo-liberalism and Neo-classical economics.

The somewhat disquieting conclusion from these reflections might lead us to proclaim that not only is business as Capital, unproductive for societal wealth, but that Business Schools as the entrenchment of Capital are likewise harmful for society in this guise.

That being said there are formulations of business and indeed Capital that are not of this unproductive semblance. The work of David Ellerman, for example, can show us how what he calls the *Democratic Firm* can resolve those issues highlighted by John Locke such that *Compacts* no longer transfer the reward of one man's labour into the pocket of another.

Insight 75:
Notes from *Capital as Business*

CasP Forum
Nitzan and Bichler (N&B) conflate business interests as conflictual to society, with the notion of sabotage. They relate this to the expansion of Capital. Their work also illustrates the correlation between the rate of profit and the level of unemployment. When N&B graph profit against business activity, could this be used to show the equivalency of Capital and business?

Islamic Economics
Islamic Finance methods could possibly provide a non-sabotaging business format by their adoption of a non interest bearing formulation of Capital. Islamic style economics, with its co-operative (mutualist) forms of business (such as Takaful) provide a non-sabotaging business form.

Financialisation
Interest as the remuneration of (Moneyed) Capital equates to profits as the reward for business. The proposition that the rates of profits and Interest rate tend to equalise could also be seen as evidence of an equivalency between Capital and business.

Marx
Marx equated Hodgskin's identification of the impossibility of the sustainability of compounded interest, with his own discussions on the inevitability of a tendency for a falling rate of profit (in *Theories of Surplus Value*). Does this amount to a tacit equivalency of Capital with business?

Insight 76:
Notes on Labour and Capital.

J.B. Clark wrote that the product was being produced by the agency of "labor and fixed Capital" (Clark [*Recent Theories of Wages*], 1883, p.354).

Thus, circulating Capital was not a productive agent, but solely an enabling force that facilitated the combination of Labour and Capital.

However, the product needs to be distributed between all three (Labour, fixed Capital and circulating Capital). Therefore, the share to both Labour and fixed Capital is diminished, whilst circulating capital is apparently allocated an unearned remuneration. In this manner, the overall reward to capital is increased and Labour's diminished.

The rhetoric can then argue that Capital is productive (i.e. has active agency). This is a sophism then for monetary gain rather than truth. We have the distinction between what is *Natural* compared with *Convention*.

It is via this *Convention* that the concept of Capital's productivity has been perpetrated. Whereas, it is from a *Natural* perspective that there is the denial that Capital can actually be productive or have agency.

Insight 77:
Capitalisation Reconciliation

Would it be possible to reconcile the following Capitalisation concepts?

a) The Post-Keynesian notion that Capitalists determine the Capital/Wages proportions of Output.

With:

b) Kalecki's idea that "workers spend what they earn, and Capitalists earn what they spend".

Joan Robinson Contention

Joan Robinson contended that Capitalists had sufficient tacit power, in their control of production's output, to decide how much of their production was retained, as capital, for future production.

Thereby they were effectively able to decide the volume of their products they made available to the Market and hence available for general use and consumption as Real Wages.

This is expressed in Austrian Economics as the decisions tacitly made by producers as to which goods produced are Goods of the First Order or alternatively Goods of a Higher Order. These decisions are obviously not made by the jobbing labourers.

As such Capitalism is a system whereby the inequitable acquisition of wealth is determined by the few that control the majority of society's wealth. Consequently producing a system of imperfect competition. This imperfect competition produces the monopolies and monopsonies that enables and facilitates the continued exploitation of the majority of society, by the minority who have secured the vast majority of the world's wealth and resources.

Kalecki Contention

When a house is brought with credit (mortgage), the money is spent or paid to clear the credit embedded within the house, so that as the credit is repaid, the value spent is transferred into the asset. The owner of the house spent X amount to acquire the asset which is of X value.

The expenditure results in the acquisition of an asset of equivalent value. The acquisition has involved no consumption or effective loss of resources, by the acquiring agent. So, when Kalecki expressed the idea that "Capitalists earn what they spend, but workers spend what they earn" he was giving expression to the concepts that:

a) Workers are effectively only ever paid subsistence wages (in line with the Iron Law of Wages). As such, effectively by definition, workers consume all that they can afford to purchase.

b) Capitalists (or the *Rich*), on the other hand, although they also consume a certain proportion of their wealth upon their necessary and discretionary subsistence, the vast majority of their revenue and/or resources can be spent or utilised upon non-consumption goods. As such the majority of their income is used to acquire additional assets or further profits. The additional utility is created for them by their exchanges.

Insight 78:
What is Capital? – A Querist

Is it the machines that help us make things? Is it the Money that allows us to buy those machines?

Who then owns the machines? Is it those that finance them?

If Capital is the money that pays for the workers' wages, who then "owns" the workers?

Who owns what the machines make? Who owns what the workers make?

Is Capital a factor of production? What makes it different to the other factors of production?

What is Land? Is Land Capital

What is Labour? Is Labour a form of Capital?

Are Wages Capital? Is Rent paid Capital?

What distinguishes Fixed from Circulating Capital?

Is a fund of money Capital? Is money a factor of production? Does money own what it pays for? Does money confer property rights?

Section 6
Money

Insight 79:
Money

Money needs to be understood as the transport (transfer) system or processes of an economy.

A significant and sustaining purpose of economic life is to process our energies, with the overall aim of improving our energy efficiency. Expressed another way, we seek to transfer our work into the consumables that improve our well-being, or wealth. Thus, money tends to be initially adopted and adapted to this transfer (barter) of goods and services between individuals for the general betterment of all.

The mistake is to conceive money simply as the vehicles within that system, and then to conceive that the more vehicles will necessarily improve that system. Just increasing the vehicles does not necessarily increase the throughput of traffic. Indeed, the traffic will slow down if there are too many vehicles. The velocity of vehicles passing through a channel will, after a certain point, decrease with an increase of the number of vehicles attempting to pass through that channel.

Money is the lifeblood of the economy, but it is not life. However, when this fundamental purpose is lost sight of, attention is concentrated more on the attainment of the vehicles (or instruments) that are conventionally used as money rather than those consumables that actually improve wealth.

In Marxist terms, attention is turned to, or refocused upon, the *Money Form* rather than the *Commodity Form*. Commodities become the intermediaries of money accumulation [i.e. MCM] rather than Money remaining the mere transitional tool between commodities' consumption [i.e. CMC].

A Fallacy of Composition creates the illusion that increases in nominal money will necessarily improve wealth. A Fallacy of Concrete Abstraction further allows for the abstract construct of money to be falsely conceived as attaining a concreteness that it does not genuinely embody.

The secret (if one can call it that), to wealth is to control the processes and thus the system of money. To control its velocity and efficiency at wealth transmission, rather than simple acquisition of nominal volumes of money.

Too much of the vehicle or instruments is not only a distraction to real economic well-being, but actually forms a barrier to industry, as well as to wealth's creation and distribution.

Insight 80:
Money in the Modern Economy

Given that in a modern economy, all money is bank credit, as all money is bank created loans, then all money in that system must amount to the commercial banks' asserts. Then, given that the bulk of these assets are created without corresponding real assets, money as such is a fictitious asset without any real-world equivalence.

To break out from this inevitable circularity we need to re-evaluate our monetary base onto a concrete asset. To avoid the asymmetry of power, and its subsequent problems, that new asset must be something each and every one can create. Not without limit, but to economic effect.

Money, on another hand, is effectively equivalent to circulating capital. As such, as Thomas Hodgskin wrote, this equates to the faith we have that whilst we work others are working to produce the commodities that we will have to exchange for the commodities we ourselves are producing, i.e. co-existing Labour (or production).

Obviously, this is not the case when that commodity is money, but solely consumable goods or services.

If money equates to trust then the assets that banks have amounts to our trust. All this trust must be conjoined into a formal form that we now recognise as money. We effectively trust that the banks' mechanisms are such as to ensure that this co-existing system of production will produce what we desire of it. Thereby, the management of our expectations of it is crucial.

When a bank creates money, when it creates credit, it is effectively creating the belief in this co-existing production. When a debt is paid off, money is destroyed in the sense that the production has been completed or consumed and as such, the belief has been completed or fulfilled.

What is necessary to ensure more production is the confidence that more production will be necessary and thereby fruitful. More money is the manifestation of that confidence.

The conservative attitude, that the past is worth conserving, as it must be better than the future, thus becomes a self-serving and self-fulfilling prophecy. Economic growth is borne of faith in others and ourselves. The conservative attitude must be born of a fear of others and the future. This in turn is borne of a recognition of being positioned better than most and thereby with something, differentially to lose.

Economic success is, when confidence in its continuation wanes, a possible negative attribute. This waning is, perhaps, often the recognition of an element of exploitation of others or the recognition that differential success (accumulation) is not altogether justified. Blind unjustified self-confidence may be a boon.

When money amounts to confidence in co-existing productive capacity it is a good thing - itself a productive good or commodity. When money mutates into the power over the productive capacities of others it becomes an exploitative bad – i.e. Capital. In the former guise, it is to be encouraged. It is from the latter guise that Labour needs to be defended.

Insight 81:
What Money Might Be?

Money has been viewed in various ways. We can illustrate these thus:

a) Any commodity used as a common means of exchange; such as gold, silver, or salt.

b) A token for a commodity, such as one described above, that is generally accepted in lieu, as a means of exchange.

c) A credit note, such as a bill of exchange or any other tradeable financial instrument or asset, generally acceptable as a means of exchange.

d) Labour, either as direct or indirect modes of exchange, or calculation (e.g. socially necessary labour).

e) Permissions to purchase; such as credit cards, overdrafts and bank deposits.

In the case of the first three above, these can all co-exist in the same economy and generally evolve in various forms, and as such are generally co-emergent with a developing market economy. They effectively form aids to the numerous and various acts of barter that are cultivated within social economies.

Although it might be assumed that commodity money predates the latter forms, there is much to support the idea that, particularly in a social or domestic economy, credit evolved as the initial monetary form. Commodity money would have developed when trade emerged between less social or alien trading partners, were trust needed to be established prior to the use of credit could be deemed acceptable.

Adam Smith referred to the relationship between money and Labour:

> Labour was the first price, the original purchase-money that was paid for all things. It was not by gold or by silver, but by labour, that all the wealth of the world was originally purchased; (Smith, *WN*, 1.5.2)

In this sense, some economists, particularly Post Keynesians, state that *Money is no means of Payment*. What they mean by this is that everyone has to work[14] to produce goods and services and receive remuneration for their labour. Thus, to purchase any commodity one must exchange one's labour, albeit via a monetary intermediate form. Where people do not actually labour but do acquire commodities, somebody else must still have originally laboured to produce those commodities.

In this way, we have a barter system and money is just an intermediary between labour and consumption. Money thereby becomes comprehended as that which enables economic agents to acquire commodities in the final act of purchase.

There is then some debate as to whether money has purposes other than being this means of exchange. These other uses can be summarised thus:

Unit of Account: Money is thus used as a measure of account despite its inevitable problematical issues as a

---

[14] As Adam Smith explains in his *Wealth of Nations*: Book I, Chapter V - *Of the Real and Nominal Price of Commodities, or of their Price in Labour, and their Price in Money.*

merely nominal, rather than real, expression of value. Monetary units of measure (i.e. fiat currencies) are presumed to be perfectly stable in real value within Historical Cost Accounting, in order to present a stable measuring unit. Monetized priced indexed tables are used to index monetary values when it is required to maintain the purchasing power or constant real value of monetary values across otherwise unstable periods.[15]

Store of Value: Whist being at one point the ability to spend and consume, money is also the ability not to consume. The utility of money is said to be its power to grant consumption, yet at the same time its power also lies in deferred or non-consumption. The utility of a means of exchange is an indirect utility, as it is the utility of what is exchanged that is of issue rather than the utility of the intermediary. However, as a store of value it acquires direct utility which compromises its indirect intermediary utility[16]

The more money functions as a store of value the more its use as a means of exchange is compromised or diminished. As J.R. Hicks finalised in his *Utility of Money* (1933), money's utility stems from the protection it offers against uncertainty. Money's Utility comes from not spending it, rather than from its being spent. The demand for money is only present in conditions of uncertainty, and is a demand for a stock of wealth.

There is an argument that money has the ability to act as a standard of deferred payment. However, as a means of exchange money can fulfil this function as an

---

[15] The presumption that price indexes can thus appropriately represent changes in monetary values is rarely challenged.
[16] This could be seen as a dialectic concept with the indirect utility as the thesis to the antithesis of its direct utility – which leads to a new synthesis for Money?

exchange across time. To specify money as a mode of fulfilling deferred payments i.e. debts it is simply a temporal means of exchange if we perceive debts as time preference based exchanges.

Mises, in his *Theory of Money and Credit* (1912)[17], made the point that strictly speaking money is not a means of payment, and used the settlement of debts as an exemplar.

Money As Trust

Money can be conceived as the trust of future Labour productively being carried out, so as to provide what will be a marketable output. Money, in this sense, is paid in leu of that output. Thus, money is a time related discount on the expected value of that output.

As a store of past labour, it is effectively redundant. Power relations will colour not only the bargaining negotiations but also the expectations as regards alternative expected valuations.

---

[17] We use the 1953 English translation herein. See Insight 83.

Insight 82:
Money, Banks and Profits

Thesis = Banks create money for the benefit of the economy and business.

Antithesis = Only banks and financial institutions effectively make profits.[18]

Synthesis = Banks only create money so they can extract profits from the economy and its businesses.

---

[18] Given Perfect Competition.

Insight 83:
Money in the Facilitation of Credit

To be consistent with the function of money as a medium of exchange, credit transactions can be considered simply as facilitating the trading of present and future commodities. However, concerns arise with the inconsistencies of nominal money's value over time compared with the *real* value of money debts. Concentration on this volatility's impact on current debt relations detracts attention from their other importance issues.

Independent Transactions
The indirect exchange of the two ultimate consumption goods is subdivided into two separate (credit based) exchanges so that the sale and purchase elements appear independent. The transaction's two elements need not be performed simultaneously. The trade's final settlement of the credit activity is disconnected from the acquisition of the final commodity.

The disengagement of the credit arrangement form the exchange results in the two parts of an otherwise single transaction being deemed as two unconnected actions. Payment of the debt obligation becomes viewed as an independent legal act. Thereby, money can legally be viewed as having the attribute of being a common medium of payment, which is obviously incorrect from an economic perspective.

Much of this economic fallacy originates with an uncritical acceptance of legal conceptions and habits of thought. Legally, outstanding debt is considered in isolation and without reference to the original obligation to pay. In Law, as in economics, money is the common medium of exchange, however the principal legal concerns with money are the problems of payment.

Law seeks to answer the question "What is money?" in order to determine how monetary liabilities can be discharged. For the jurist, money is thus a medium of payment.

The economist, to whom the problem of money presents a different aspect, should not adopt this point of view if they do not want to confuse their understanding . of economic reality.

> For the jurist, money is a medium of payment. The economist, to whom the problem of money presents a different aspect, may not adopt this point of view if he does not wish at the very outset to prejudice his prospects of contributing to the advancement of economic theory. (Mises, 1953, p.37)

Insight 84:
The New Financial Economic Reality

The financial world, like any other environment, is subject to continuous change and development. This can be seen, for example, in the evolution of Financialisation as more and more, what traditionally would have been conceived as non-financial institutions are transformed, via the expediency of market pressures, into increasingly financial firms. The operational advantages of perceiving profits as the growth in net assets, rather than the difference betwixt income and expenditure, propels more companies down to path to apparent financial institution-hood.

What was once seen as at the cutting-edge of financial economics is now really the common place. Students are no longer surprised by a revelation that firms are increasingly becoming equivalent or akin to financial institutions in their commercial operations.

Within the traditional relationship between firms and households, not only has the firm evolved, but so too has the other partner in the circular flow of funds via the financial intermediaries. It should be recognised by economists that households have mutated. The ideal of the household as the traditional Ultimate Lender is no longer realistic. The idea that the majority or even a significant proportion of households can run their financial affairs so as to achieve a persistent surplus should seem an obvious fallacy.

The evidence shows that households' debt levels were in March 1918 running at £119bn annually.[19]

Some commentators point out that households are now debt-fuelled given the stagnation (if not real decline) in wages.

In this new reality, both firms and households are Ultimate Borrowers. This being the case, who now fills the increasingly necessary role of Ultimate Lenders?

The perhaps obvious answer would be the banks. It is now recognized, not least by the Bank of England, that the banks are the creators of our currency, by means of their lending activities.

In this manner, banks have evolved themselves from being just intermediaries in the flow of funds (between firms and households) to the supreme role of Ultimate Lenders (to both firms and households). All other parties in the economy have become dependent upon the banks. Banks have gone from being too big to fail to an even far more controlling position, so that our very (continued) existence is subject to the banks' permissions.

If households have become Ultimate Borrowers, does this mean that they have ceased being risk adverse and adopted a more risk loving or taking stance?

It is, perhaps, an inevitability that households should have become Ultimate Borrowers given that banks can create money *ex nihilo*. The economic flow of funds still flows between Ultimate Borrowers and Lenders, but in an apparent act of efficiency, there is now no longer a need for intermediaries.

---

[19] ONS report - Household debt in Great Britain: April 2016 to March 2018 released 5th December 2019 (p.2)

That is not to say that those that had acted as intermediaries no longer exist, just that they have changed their role. These former intermediaries no longer have to depend on the external supply of (deposited) funds coming from Ultimate Lenders (Households and/or Savers), but have manipulated the situation so they themselves have usurped the former Ultimate Lenders.

Not only this, but the manoeuvring has effectively forced the previous Ultimate Lenders to transform themselves into Ultimate Borrowers.

One could also wonder whether this latter transformation was a necessary and sufficient condition actively sought or just an inevitable outcome given the previous events and conditions.

If the rate of profit is a percentage return on a nominal amount of money invested, and this money is a creation of credit: then (logically) the rate of profit is related to the creation of credit.

As such, the economist should have some understanding of this relationship. One particular issue, however, is that the creation of credit itself is in some way related to the expected or assumed rate of return on the nominal form of money lent.

It might be reasonable to expect the amount of credit granted to increase as the expected returns themselves increase. Indeed, the Law of Supply and Demand should, perhaps, lead us to expect the demand for credit (and hence money) to increase as the expected rate of return increases.

If we relate the expected future rate of return to the current rate of profit, it is not unreasonable to conceive a correlation between the creation of credit and the current rate of profit. An appropriate question then emerges:

Does the rate of profit depend on the amount of credit money created or *vice versa*?

One thing that becomes clear however, is that the nominal rate of profit is no longer exclusively dependent upon the productivity of the enterprises entered into. The profit rate has become determinable by those that grant credit. Given that we might reasonably assume there is always an excessive demand for credit with regards to its supply.

One could perhaps imagine that leaving such an important power as being the determinant of credit and thereby profit in the hands of private institutions or individuals, would be an irresponsible policy for any Government to adopt.

Whilst it might be reasonable to argue that no government can determine the demand for money in a free market economy, does this mean the power over the rate of profit and who makes it can be safely left in the hands of admittedly self-serving individual economic agents?

There is also an issue with capital becoming even more the power to grant credit and money. This equivalency between money and capital also further clarifies the notion of Capital as Power, when money is economically recognized as permission to spend.

Liam Byrne famously left a letter on the desk of incoming minister (Treasury Secretary) David Laws, saying "Dear Chief Secretary, I'm afraid to tell you there's no money left,". The idea that money can run out when money is credit would mean that credit had run out or been exhausted. What does it mean if a government or an economy has run out of credit?

It is the flows of lending funds, which keep the pool topped up; that enables banks to engage in fractional reserve banking activities. The velocity increases but the actual absolute (nominal) remains unchanged or actually lessens.

The quantity of borrowing can therefore be understood as disconnected from the level of (absolute) deposits.

Insight 85:
Money as a Commodity

If money is considered as a commodity, then the world's wealth [ω] considered as the sum of the commodities within it must include the sum of all money therein.

Thus the world's wealth could be considered as the sum of wealth in the form of money [ω^m] plus the sum of all non-money commodities [ω^g] – calling these non-money commodities *goods* for convenience.

$$\omega = \omega^m + \omega^g$$

Hence, with each additional quantum of money, the world's wealth as a whole must increase. However, as each individual can only possess a finite sum of that wealth with each addition of money, each individual's share of that whole wealth must diminish.

$$\Delta\omega^m = \Delta\omega, \quad \text{but } \Delta\omega^g = 0$$

Thereby, as the proportion of money increases within the whole wealth, the fraction of wealth in goods must diminish:

$$\Delta\omega^m/\omega > 0 \quad \therefore \quad \Delta\omega^g/\omega < 0$$

If money is seen as a non-consumable commodity, then the share of wealth we have diminishes as the share of consumable wealth we have access to also contracts.

If the changes in money were exactly proportional to the changes in other commodities:

$$\text{If } \Delta\omega^m/\omega = \Delta\omega^g/\omega$$

Then, as the changes to whole wealth would also equate to these dimensions, there would be no changes to relative wealth.

Insight 86:
Money Illusion and Crises

Money Illusion and its most closely associated Economic Paradigm, Mercantalism, are both consequences of a Fallacy of Concrete Abstraction. Money, in both instances, is mistakenly perceived, or assumed to be a stock, and consequently treated as such, rather than a process (or flow).

Money becomes a variable that can be accumulated, and wealth is seen erroneous as improved simply when its stock numerically increases. It is the confusion of riches for wealth.

By analogy, money is akin to a river, where everyone values the water so much that they remove and keep stock quantities of it on their own patch of land for fear that others will do likewise, and so the river will dry up. It becomes a self-fulfilling prophecy as the river runs dry because too much has been removed from its flow.

Once this disastrous state is recognised, the authorities pump loads more water back into the stream in the hope that it will eventually return to being a river. However, if the real nature of water (i.e. money) is not understood or learnt, the cycle of deprivation will simply repeat itself in a cycle of crises.

As such, financial crises are endemic in modern capitalism. Only by acknowledging the Process Philosophical view of the economy and thereby money, can we hope to break these moribund cycles of wax and wane.

In contrast to such a resolution, the present methodological individualistic fallacies persist. Those number of those whose stock is periodically improved by these crises will be diminished. However, as these limited few are increasingly enriched and further empowered, the majority, in contrast, are further impoverished.

It is not in the interest of this diminishing elite to promulgate the demise of the Fallacy of Concrete Abstractions whilst its consequences persist in enriching them.

They themselves may well be victims of this fallacy in their misguided faith in their security, but they too have mistaken riches for wealth. As their numbers decrease, as money is increasingly concentrated in the hands of fewer protagonists.

This systemic malfeasance is sustained by another illusion - *the Survival of the Fittest.* When Darwin wrote about this, he did not mean that the strongest, or in some way best, survived. In evolutionary terms survival depends upon a species fitting successfully within the particular niche in which it finds itself.

Square pegs fit in square holes. They are not fundamentally better than round pegs, they just happen to better fit a specific environment. However, the *Survival of the Fittest* illusion convinces those that are rich, that there must be something superior about them, which justifies their elevated social position. They believe they are the cream that rises to the top.

Unfortunately, this delusion is promulgated throughout society, and people tend to accept a meritorious respect and legitimacy to their "betters". After all, a certain cognitive dissonance makes this easier to live with and accept, than the arbitrary randomness that really characterises social realities and relationships.

Insight 87:
Saving as an Externality

As an alternative perspective, one could understand that when a stock is created out of a flow, this stock is effectively an externality to all but those which hold that stock. Stock, as property, is thereby a negative externality for everyone in the economy.

In a like manner *Saving* is effectively an externality, in that the costs are not borne by the perpetrator, but only by everybody else. Given that everyone is thus suffering by the multitudinous acts of saving within the economy, we are all suffering from these externalities.

Insight 88:
Ownership of Money

If there is no such thing as money, or we acknowledge money as a flow, can the expression "My Money" be valid?

If money is "no means of Payment", the alleged ownership of money is a substitute for the ownership of that which is a "means of payment" i.e. [in the main] Labour.

The ownership of money is thereby *de jure* the ownership of the Labourers and thus tantamount to institutionalised Slavery.

Money, *de facto*, is simply an exchange medium that is a socially shared, so as to facilitate exchanges of labour and its products within an economy (society).

Insight 89:
Money as a Service

Money is not something someone can own. Rather it is a service one can make use or misuse of. Alternatively, money's ownership is an inclusive, rather than exclusive possession in use.

So when, legally, we do not own (i.e. exclusively) the money in our bank accounts it is because the banks also have inclusive property, in use, of that same asset.

As such money tends not to be exclusively owned, particularly as the majority of money exists as non-cash forms, such as bank deposits and credit (loans, overdrafts, and credit cards) and numerous other bank assets. In fact, the vast bulk of money exists as derivatives.

Indeed, from this perspective, money exists as credit, which is a reification of trust - which in turn is concatenated (multi-layered) inclusively rather than exclusively.

This makes the accurate quantification of money (nearly?) impossible. As a single quantum of money exists at many levels, and can be instantaneously used and experienced by alternative users at any single moment of its being.

Insight 90:
The Price of Money

If by price we mean the exchange ratio of two goods, then what does the expression that "interest is the price of money" mean?

When every day we talk about Prices, we are using the notion of Money Prices, whereby money, as the means of exchange, is the notional good in which all other goods are expressed in ratio with.

Thus, to have any cogent meaning, Interest as the "*price*" of money must be something other than the ratio of money to money, as effectively this would be just an empty identity.

Undoubtedly, though the intention is to express a monetary notion of price in regard to money. This can only make sense when our two goods are distinctly diverse formulations of money. As such, the two formulations must be distinguished temporally.

Interest is the ratio of money at one given point in time with itself at a different point.

$$I = M(^{t}){:}M(^{t+n})$$

If the Capital and money markets are only dealing in the same good, but simply differentiated over time, then both are effectively concerned with interest, and Capital and money are only distinguishable in terms of time preferences.

The question then arises as to what is being traded? A logical conclusion can be that it is power, primarily in the sense of economic power. Time and Liquidity Preferences can thereby be understood as preferences as to when to exercise that economic power.

Those with no store or stock of economic power must seek out economic power for immediate purposes (survival in the extreme). Those with a relative excess of immediate economic power have the luxury of being able to exercise their time/liquidity preferences.

Thus, the economy becomes characterised in terms of asymmetric power, manifested in monetary terms and evident in asymmetric Capital distribution.

Insight 91:
A Money Theory of Property

A Money Theory of Property is such that all property is definable in monetary terms. This is a requirement of a system were exchange, especially commodity exchange, is based on the fungibility of property, particularly in terms of money. This in turn is a requirement of an economic system that promotes and promulgates the accumulation of alienated property.

In such a system all property is alienable, and definable (i.e. fungible with) in monetary terms. The prime property that needs to be accepted in these terms, is Labour. In order for a system to be supportive of partisan accumulation of wealth, it is necessary for Labour to be exchangeable in monetary terms, especially within a market economy.

The concepts of inclusive property and thereby inclusive ownership have to be replaced solely by individualistic ownership facilitating exclusive property rights. Inclusive property rights are incompatible with alienable fungible commodities and hence exchange economies.

The alternative, whereby Labour is inalienable, does not facilitate the accumulation of property. The fungibility of property with money, is also a requirement. In a market economy it is imperative that all property (both inclusive and exclusive) is conceived as fungible, and that Labour is accepted as simply another alienable commodity that is likewise monetarily fungible.

The idea of inalienable but inclusive (i.e. social) Labour and property rights is an anathema to market economics.

When Polanyi expressed the Marginalist Revolution as the attempt to embed society within the economy (rather than the economy being simple embedded within society), such a Monetary Theory of Property and the commoditization of alienated Labour are effectively both prerequisites.

Insight 92:
A Note on the Expansion of the Amount of Money

Within a closed economic system, for the money prices of goods and services to stay within the same relative proportions, the increase in the amount of money together with the increase in the amount of those goods and services, must be in the same relative proportions.

For example, if the amount of goods and services increases by 10% and the amount of money within that economy also increases by 10% (within the same period) there should be no change in the relative money prices for those goods.

However, the *Quantity Theory of Money* (QTM), in an initial simply iteration, would lead to the understanding that if the amount of money were to be expanded by 11%, whilst the amount of goods and service (output) upon which it was to be expended only improved by 10%, then there would be more money available to be exchanged for those goods and services. In such a situation, assuming that the Law of Supply and Demand was holding there would be more units of money available for each quanta or item of good or service. The resulting position would be that as more money was available and competitive forces were operative, the Money Prices of all those goods and service would, on an overall average, increase so as to utilize the available money funds. To paraphrase Parkinson's Law, - The Prices of goods expands to meet the money available.

The logic of the QTM can also be applied to falls in output and in the money supply, as well increases in Output without changes to the quantity of money. For example, an increase in overall productivity in output, unaccompanied by a change in the amount of money, would lead to less money chasing increased goods and services so as the reduce overall average money prices within an economy. This would effectively be money Price deflation and, by many economists, would be seen as somewhat less than positive despite the effective overall increase in social Income resulting.

The alignment of overall Income and Output is also important when considering the price implications of money supply changes. In our relatively simplistic presentation of QTM we have implied that all goods and services produced will be circulated within an economy so as to be exchanged with money. In this way everything produced (output) is to be consumed and used as individuals' income. In a way this is a useful picture that equals a society's wealth with its productive capabilities. Indeed, it is that used by Adam Smith at the very beginning of his *Wealth of Nations* (1776):

> The annual labour of every nation is the fund which originally supplies it with all the necessaries and conveniences of life which it annually consumes, and which consist always either in the immediate produce of that labour, or in what is purchased with that produce from other nations.
>
> According therefore as this produce, or what is purchased with it, bears a greater or smaller proportion to the number of those who are to consume it, the nation will be better or worse

supplied with all the necessaries and conveniences for which it has occasion.

When the amount of money is increased without a correspondingly proportional increase in output, the nominal prices of available output will be appropriately increased.

This increase in money will have no effect on the overall level of output (or as such, wealth), but will have distributional affects upon who can consume the output.

One other effect of an increase in money following on from the re-distribution is that those that are in receipt of proportionality more will consume a lower proportion of their nominal income on goods or less on real income.

Those that subsequently receive proportionally less nominal income, will thereby receive less real income.

The overall effect is that less real income will be consumed. An increase in money, that is not universally equal, will result in a lower consumption of real income, which amounts to less wealth being utilised.

Insight 93:
A *New* basis for Financial Relationship

Our present financial relationships are based on *money* being lent to people. Effectively people rent themselves in exchange for money. Would it be possible to have relationships based on money and capital being rented by people? This would change the power relationship between those in control of capital and money with those having the need or requirement for the finance.

If our industrial relationships changed such that Capital could no longer rent (i.e. temporarily own) Labour, then the whole social nature of Capitalist relationships would necessary be changed. Such a change within employment relationships would inevitably have implications for the overall role of Capital in society.

At present finance is framed within power relationships that are parallel to those in employment arrangements. Effectively if we wish to charge the power asymmetry in the latter, it will also be necessary to do so in the former.

If we conceive a society where Labour hires Capital, then Capital becomes the tool of Labour; rather than Labour being the tool of Capital. Likewise, Capital must function as a tool of people in all aspects, not just in the employment sphere.

In financial terms payments for funds need to be (one off) fees for use rather than compounded interest payments. The problems of Capital's all engrossing power stems from its ability to command compounded interest. It therefore requires a curtailment or reversal of these arrangements to correct these problems.

Capital must be returned to being the servant of humanity, rather than being the Master of society.

Insight 94:
Finance through Money Creation Banking

Given that banks can create money ex nihilo: - Does the price elasticity of money (as interest) determine the amount that will/can be created? Is it really money that is the goal of money creation?

Banks' profits relate to their receiving interest? If so, less money created will result in higher interest rates, and presumably higher profits?

The Intermediation of Loanable Funds (ILF) model of Money creation is based on the fiction of a barter system. In contrast, the Monetary System view (e.g. of Graziani) allows for the Finance through Money Creation (FMC) model.

Within a barter system, we might well have had a ILF system; but once we progressed into a truly monetary system, we must necessarily be within a FMC form. Does the implementation of FMC lead to the monetary system, or visa versa? Or were the FMC and the transition away from barter co-established so as to consolidate and further the power status of banks, financiers, and the general power elite?

Insight 95:
Notes on Bank Reserves and The Money Multiplier Mystery

Bank Reserves

There are two distinct forms of Reserves that commercial banks can be asked to hold.

The first form, known just as Bank Reserves or Cash Reserve Ratio, are the reserves held in relation to their deposits. This is the money banks need to hold against what their account holders might wish to withdraw. Many central banks impose specific requirements upon their associated commercial banks in this regard. The Bank of England does not, but rather relies on the banks' own commercial operational judgements.

The other form of Reserves are the Capital Reserve requirements, held to international agreements, in relation to banks' assets; their loans and other assets.

The BoE paper – "The Framework of Capital Requirements for UK Banks" (Dec. 2015) relates to these latter requirements, i.e. not the Cash Reserves.

So, when it is said that the BoE, unlike for example the Federal Reserve, do not impose Reserve ratios, this is true, but not to say Capital adequacy Requirements are not in place. These are technically different entities.

It is generally accepted (for numerous technical reasons) that Capital Adequacy Requirements do not (directly) affect the money Supply. Only Cash Reserves can influence the money supply, which is why some central banks impose Cash Reserve Ratios. The BoE does not use this tool to control the money supply, but relies on its Discount (Bank) Rate and its Open Market Operations (OMO).

Money Multiplier Mystery.
The term, Money Multiplier, is used in two distinct modes.

One is an abstract process whereby funds deposited into a bank account are successively let out, at a consistent reserve ratio. Thus, the total deposits created following a nominal single (original) deposit can be calculated. Thereby, this is merely a synthetic *a priori* proposition.

The other one is an empirically discernible change in the amount of money circulating within an economy following an original investment. As such this is a synthetic *a posteriori* proposition.

The former can be seen as an abstract process within an economy, whereas the latter is claimed to be a measurable variable. They are somewhat related, but are nevertheless quite distinct.

The abstract process is (for some) theoretically formulated as a formal explanation of the variable. The BoE are thus denying the validity of the theoretical process, whilst still representing the (empirical) variable. The BoE use the FMC (Finance through Money Creation) explanation to explain the variable, as it appears more empirically validated.

However, if we want to be really accurate even this explanation could be criticised philosophically. What is classed as a variable is simply an abstraction and thereby a synthetic *a priori* proposition. As such, it is, in modern parlance, thingified so to make it appear as an entity that can thereby be used and validated within a science. Effectively, by adopting the fallacy of concrete abstraction, it is erroneously transfigured from a synthetic *a priori* proposition into an analytical proposition.

Without this transformation, this abstraction could not be considered as an entity within Economics. Regrettably this process of thingification, the practice of creating entities from abstractions, is widespread throughout economics, and modern science generally. One result of which, albeit one of the least damaging, is illustrated by the confusion often experienced regarding these terms.

We would hope this explanation can go some way to someday clarifying this issue.

Insight 96:
Interest

Interest is different things to different people; indeed, it is different things in different contexts. In this way, it can be seen as typical of the components that populate the economic world. For economics to be a discipline it would seem appropriate if we had specific and definitive terms. In reality, however, this is never going to be the case, particularly for its most important terms.

Different schools of thought thus answer the question "what is interest?" with different conclusions. It would seem that these various schools necessarily have different definitions of *Interest* because they have different ideas of what *Money* is or should be.

Once we have resolved the issue of *money* we can begin to better understand *Interest*.

A common solution is to view interest as the price of money. However, this then highlights further our nomenclature problems. Money itself is a far from concrete term.

If price is taken as a ratio of exchange between two items we have numerous manifestations of money. The *Corn* Price is the amount of corn exchangeable for any other good. The *Labour* Price equates to the amount of Labour that must be exchanged to receive another good.

Our social conventions usually resolve such that a particular good becomes the widely accepted means of exchange. Thereby money becomes the ubiquitous form of exchange, initially with some relatively constant and persistent value, but eventually settled as a merely token worth. Prices, and indeed value, become conventionally and conveniently expressed, as the *Money* Price, in this nominal denomination, as currency.

However, as a ratio expression, this currency must be conceived as denominator. If interest is the price of money its expression requires the same items as the two sides of the ratio; as both denominator and numerator. This leads to a logical contradiction as the *Money Price* of money.

Considered as the rental price of money, it could reveal to us that money has some form of productiveness that warrants this revenue.

Insight 97:
Non-Money Interest

Interest is more than simply adding a rate of return to original sum of money. It is to gain anything more from an activity than was input.

If, as Adam Smith said, Labour was the original money, gaining an advantage over someone else's labour is interest. As, for example, when Thomas Hodgskin claimed that Capital amounted to the control over another's labour.

Insight 98:
Low Interest Rates

Low interest rates, and the measures taken by Central Banks to maintain and lower interest rates, will artificially increase bond prices (as an identity).

Such rises in Bond prices can have various consequences:

Firstly, it fosters a certain confidence in financial markets, which manifests as higher prices for other financial instruments.

Secondly, as existing assets are thus valued higher, profits, as defined by the growth (in value) of assets are artificially raised.

Thirdly, the wealth of the asset-endowed sectors of society increases, whereas the poorer (unendowed) portions of society are further disadvantaged. The resultant increased social inequalities potentially create further economic instabilities.

Fourthly, the rise in asset values and profits encourages financial economic activity to create what might easily become a bubble, to the longer-term detriment of the economy.

A fifth consequence may well be that all these financial activities detrimentally draws funds away from the real sectors of the economy. This worsens the physical aspects of the economy, encourages additional Financialisation, and thus further unbalances and destabilises the economy.

All these consequences are effectively counter to the original measures' intentions.

Insight 99:
Profit and Loss Sharing

When a loan is made from a financial institution to an economic agent the financial institution is not responsible for what the economic agent does with the sum involved. The financial institution has an interest in insuring that the economic agent will be able to maintain their ability to repay their financial commitment to the financial institution and may take out appropriate guarantees such as second charges upon a house in the case of a mortgage.

If the economic agent uses the funds in, for example, a business enterprise and losses those funds the obligation of the economic agent still remains to financial institution. The economic agent is still expected to repay their debt to the financial institution.

However, the financial institution has no claims on any financial gain made by the economic agent via their use funds. So, for example, in the case of a business loan, the financial institution has no claim on the profits made as a result of a loan made to finance an economic agent's business enterprise.

As such payments made into a financial institution by an investor are a similar loan arrangements, whether these payments are nominally deposits, insurance premiums, or payments for any other financial services or investments.

If the funds placed by an *investor* remained the *investor*'s property then the financial institution could not loan them out to another economic agent without sustaining an obligation to share their gains made by their financing activities. Thus, deposits need to be legally loans to the banks, so that the banks can use its customers' (depositors' or investors') funds without reference or obligations to the depositors. On the other side, it ensures that the depositors suffer no obligations due to the banks' losses on unfulfilled loans.

In Islamic *Profit & Loss* arrangement both the financial institution and economic agent share the obligations of financing. If a bank provides 5% of the funds for a particular enterprise then if that business suffers a loss, then the Islamic bank will forfeit 5% of the funds they advanced. Likewise, if there is an operating profit, then the financial institution would receive 5% of those gains.

Insight 100:
Securities Lending

Securities lending is a technique whereby one party who owns a security "lends" it to another party (for a specific period). The borrower exchanges collateral with the lender as a guarantee for the lent security.

The borrower's immediate purpose is to sell it. The reason for selling it (at the time the deal is made) is that the borrower believes that they that can sell what has been lent to them and then subsequently buy it or an equivalent item back at a lower price when they are due to return it to the original lender.

The borrower therefore believes that there is a profit to be made by initially selling an item before buying it back at a later lesser price. The differential between the two prices over the time period involved, is the determining potential profit rate.

The lender's position is covered by the borrower's collateral and sets their terms to be assured of some gain, as their profit. They also entertain such a deal as, for its duration, the security involved is not classed as an asset and therefore does not have to be covered by appropriate reserves.

Section 7
Distribution

Insight 101:
A Problem for Humanity in Society.

There is a problem for humanity in society. One for which economists can justly task themselves with attempting to resolve. And this is - How can we achieve an appropriate and equitable distribution?

The economic fallacy of apparently equitable marginal distribution can only be attained within Perfect Competition, whereas Perfect Competition is only possible when distribution is equitable.[20] It is somewhat akin to a chicken and egg analogy, or perhaps the similarly incongruous notion of attaining dynamic equilibrium from a non-equilibrium static starting point. However, although Perfect Competition and equity may be necessary conditions for each other, neither is likely to be sufficient for the other.

Whilst it might be assumed that everyone may well be content with a distribution based on justice, this admirable motivation is inevitably compromised by the contradictive endowments of those already advantaged by pre-existing distributional disparities.[21]

---

[20] We need elsewhere to explain (or at least discuss) why Perfect Competition and equitable distribution are mutually necessary for each other's existence.

[21] By *Justice* we refer to the Roman notion of delivering to

Orthodox economic theorising recognises this paradox in its *Pareto Optimality*. Nevertheless, such initial endowments are always the starting point that inevitably impedes a truly equitable distribution. It is perhaps this orthodoxy's conceptualisation of humanity's individualist self-interest seeking instrumental rationality that provides the parameters that necessitate accommodation to facilitate this problem's resolution.

Indeed, it is the creed of modern orthodox economics that has championed this particular incarnation of instrumental rationality that seems crucial to resolving the distributional quandary. If we believe Karl Polanyi, as in his *The Great Transformation* (1944), it is this ideology that identifies and then utilises these impediments to equitability as a self-fulfilling prophecy of human greed.

Others, such as David Ellerman, seek solutions (Economic Democracy) via jurisprudence and a re-analysis of the *Firm*.[22] Nitzan and Bichler identify *Differential Accumulation* and the utilisation of an almost Hodgskinite concept of *Capital as Power*.[23]

The orthodoxy acknowledges its need to retreat from reality and to abstract and mathematise. This is

---

each their due and proper property (and rights).

[22] See Ellerman: *The Democratic Worker-Owned* Firm (1990) and *Property and Contract in Economics: The Case for Economic Democracy* (1992). More recently *The Labour Theory of Property and Marginal Productivity Theory* in the World Economics Association's *Economic Thought* (April 2016).

[23] We thus acknowledge the work of the 19th Century economist Thomas Hodgskin as the starting point for many of our inquiries and investigations.

countered within the Post-Autistic movement and its Real World Economics.

Thus, we have a diversity within contemporary political economy, which although pluralistic in outlook, has a propensity to oppose (or at the very least challenge) the Neo-classical economic orthodox at its philosophical and methodological cores.

If we are to address our primary quandary, not only do we need to be familiar with Polanyi's initial analysis, but also the solutions offered up by Ellerman, Nitzan & Bichler, and the Post Autistic Movement, as well as other kindred spirits.

The solution we thus seek is how to attain an equitable distribution. However, the first stumbling block on this route is how to define an equitable distribution. Especially, at question is how do we attain a universal acceptance of a conceptually *Equitable Distribution*? For without such universality it remains simply hypothetical.

The Object of Equitable Distribution

For there to be an equitable distribution we must recognise that there is something to be disseminated. Secondly, we must presume that what is to be circulated must be desired or at least required by the general populace. It is this second matter that has concentrated economists' efforts upon the issue of value.

A confounding of these two initial matters is caused by the question as to whether it is actual objects or their value that needs to be equitably distributed. If it be the objects, then this can be conceived as a somewhat objective discourse. However, once our efforts are focused on value, we have entered the realm of subjectivism.

Ideally, therefore, that which is to be the object of equitable distribution, if it is to be universally accepted, must be both objectively and subjectively satisfying. We are thus faced with another dilemma – do we seek an entity that is both objectively and subjectively acceptable? Or do we seek one that only attempts to fulfil a singular criterion that is otherwise generally acceptable as a proxy for the other.

A not uncommon approach has been to seek an objective medium that has an objective value that can thus be used to express the value of all goods, commodities, and services. Some Labour theorists have tried to align labour with such an expression in a Labour Theory of Value.[24]

Such an attempted approach can be seen in Marx's concept of *Socially Necessary Labour Time*. Marx's difficulties where subsequently addressed in Piero Sraffa's *Production of Commodities by Means of Commodities* (1960) and his *Composite Commodity*.

Neo-Classical Economics effectively denies the usefulness of these two attempts in its assertion of the supremacy of Marginalist individualistic idiosyncratic subjective valuations. However, despite the logical rejection of cardinality in favour of ordinality, modern economists still persist in the use of monetary (i.e. nominal) values as a proxy of value. For example, Lloyd Shapley's game theoretic approach to fair distribution was effectively based on the monetary endowments of the players at the onset of the *game*.

---

[24] Not to be confused with a *Labour Theory of Property*, although we will need to investigate this proposition within our inquiries.

The fluidity of the monetary medium and its inequitable asymmetrical distributional creation are highlighted in Augusto Graziani's *The Monetary Theory of Production* (2003). This work is more than just a monetary tract but emerges as a critical work of Political Economy.

Arbitrary Power Endowments.
Examples of the Neoclassicals' cardinal approach can be seen expressed within the concept of the Shapley-Shubik and Banzhaf *power indices*.

The relatively simply Shapley-Shubik power index can provide an interesting illustration with its formula:

$$P = \frac{k}{2n + 2 - k}.$$

Whereby the power [P] of the dominant agent (e.g. the capitalist) increases disproportionately as that power enlarges. This, perhaps, illustrates that distribution based on power can never really be considered (from this mathematical perspective) as fair.

However, if the distribution of rewards within production should be proportional to the power (i.e. the importance or bargaining power) of the participants, then necessarily those participants will be motivated to seek an increase in their power, so as to increase their reward (i.e. profit).

This leads to a gatekeeper problem, in that arbitrary power, in the guise of *Capital*, is sought rather than productivity. In this way Capital has assumed a mantle of prominence and a superiority that might not be otherwise warranted. Capital's economic dominance within Capitalism is due to assumed significance rather than any actual productivity.

When one ponders why Capital's productive worth is almost universally accepted one might perhaps see an answer in Behavioural Economics. Behavioural biases (for example, dispositional effects, anchoring and endowment biases) are such that unwarranted value is attached solely from long established practice.

This notion of *Naïve Productivity* identified by Böhm-Bawerk, is thereby not un-associated with economic sabotage, whereby lower productivity is sought as a means to increasing power, and hence profits. We are also here drawn into a consideration of principal–agent problems.

For a system of distribution to be equitable it should be based on the productiveness of the contributors not simply the relative power of the participants.[25] This, effectively, can be seen explored in the work of David Ellerman with his discussions of jurisprudence and the nature of the firm.

Capitalists inevitably seek to maintain their (bargaining) power through legislative instruments, and perpetuating the firm in its capitalistic form (rather than the co-operative form). Indeed, in Hodgskin's *Natural and Artificial Right of Property* (1832), it was argued that a capitalistic system couched in legal instruments is actually not only counterproductive, but also diametrically opposed to a free market economy. We can see Hodgskin's reasoning reiterated within the Austrian School's attacks on what it calls *Crony Capitalism*.[26]

---

[25] The power of the *Agents* has sovereignty over the productiveness of the *Principals*.

[26] Although some (e.g. Ben Shapiro's *There's No Such Thing as "Crony Capitalism"* (2011) effectively point out that what is often referred to as Crony Capitalism is not capitalistic but

We are thus faced with several research inquiries and some miscellaneous subsidiary issues.

Research Inquiries:
a) A definition, or at least an understanding, of what is to be distributed.   This can be equated to the economists' long sort for understanding of value.

b) A clarification of the complexion and application of arbitrary power and its endowment. In the modern economic sphere, this would include *money* as a manifestation of arbitrary power.

c) An understanding of why a *Naïve Productivity theory* still persists in maintaining Capital's power within Capitalism.

d) An understanding of the nature of the modern firm. This should be able to both identify its currently prevalent form and its *ideal* distributional form.

e) A comprehension of the inherent jurisprudence issues commensurate with Principal-Agent problems.

f) An understanding of the relational character and behaviour of what is commonly conceived of as *Capital*.

g) Establishing the subsequent economic sabotage and the associated (or resultant) *Differential Accumulation* of *Capital*.

h) Identification of Real World economic issues combined with the demarcation of the limitations of orthodox abstract economics.

---

rather a modern form of Mercantilism (Corporatism).

Some Miscellaneous Subsidiary Issues.

We also find ourselves faced with several subsidiary matters:-

- Should we consider all capitalistic or unearned profit (i.e. derived exclusively from power) simply as rent? Are we then drawn to some of the problems identified in Piketty's *Capital in the 21st Century* (2013)?

- Should we thereby acknowledge Capital, as Hodgskin explained in 1825, simply as "the power of one man over the Labour of another". Hodgskin also raised the issue of the impossibility of quantifying Capital; does this amount to a problem of the measurement of power?

- Should considerations of power and productivity be limited to the ordinal rather than the cardinal?

- If we relegate arbitrarily endowed power, are we then necessarily promoting concurrent creatively generated productive power, whether that be physical or mental labour?

- Are we then faced with a problem in being able to distinguish between productive power and non-productive power? Would this issue be akin to resurrecting the old distinction between productive and non-productive labour?[27]

---

[27] Already effectively countered by Daniel Raymond in *Thoughts on Political Economy: A Theory of Productive Power* (1820) and Robert Torrens *An Essay on the Production of Wealth* (1821).

Insight 102:
Artificial Distributions

There is a Natural Distribution that is more normally described as the Normal Distribution, with its characteristic bell curve around a "centralised point".

In contrast to this, there are Artificial Distributions that distribute around a humanistic unnatural distribution. These are artificial in the sense that they are the results of human artifice and are at variance to the Normal Distribution's centralised position.

The prime example of a humanistic or artificial distribution is the consequence of the imposition of compounded interest, in economic affairs. The basis of theological and economic antagonism towards Interest are effectively focused upon its artificial distributional effects.

After an introductory preface of the numerous issues, an effective exposition would need to explore a central mechanism that facilitates and perpetuates Artificial Distribution, which is reification, or as Alfred Whitehead expressed it, the Fallacy of Concrete Abstraction.

Apart from this exposition of the persistence of reification, we should also explore what is conceive as a Normal (i.e. randomised) Distribution. This would be necessary so as to highlight its antagonism that is Artificial Distribution.

The initial manifestation of Artificial Distribution that we should illustrate would be, perhaps, the most obvious, but generally accepted, although not universally, i.e. compounded interest. This is the ideal example as it is both an expression of reification and of distribution antagonistic towards Normal/Natural Distribution.

Insight 103:
The Division of Output Decision

If Kalecki and others are correct, and Capitalists are empowered to decide the allocation of output as either consumption or investment goods, how should this be dealt with? Should society allow such important decisions to be left in the hands of these vested self-interested factions?

These Division of Output decisions are made during production but determines distribution. However, those that make the Division of Output decisions are largely unaware and unaffected by their negative consequences. Are the Division of Output decisions made by market forces or simply by individual self-interests? They are effectively externalities, as their costs are not effectively borne by those that make them.

Could a system based on Democratic Firms (e.g. Co-operatives) address these decisions in a more socially equitable manner? Would there need to be so much of Society's output designated as investment goods (Capital) within a Democratic Firm based economy?

Does the amount of Capital created by the Division of Output decisions in a Capitalist economy become proportional to its conceptions of the pre-existing levels of Capital? Does this, in turn, relate to the resultant level of consumption goods?

When theorists, such as Thomas Hodgskin, Anton Menger, J.B. Clark, and David Ellerman, upheld the Labourers' right to the Whole [of their] Product, were they effectively declaring that the whole of society's product (i.e. its whole output) should be allocated as consumption goods?

They certainly sided with the notion of Capital's unproductiveness and the unjustified nature of capitalist profits (as unwarranted transfers away from the workers).

In an isocratic economy/society the Division of Output would presumably be more aligned with Sraffa's equations in his *Production of Commodities by Means of Commodities*.

However, as Adam Smith recognised, once Capitalism becomes established, wages will always be held down towards subsistence. The balance of power inevitably resides with the Capitalists, and thereby against the labourers.

There would seem to be a link between Say's law and the Division of Output, in that Say assumed that all outputs are necessarily sold and thereby presumably consumed. The apparent efficiency of *The Market* is that everything produced is utilised, as prices accommodate to ensure all is used. Such accommodation would also encompass the price of labour and thus its wages. In such a situation, Wages and the Prices of goods would have to effect bipartisan flexible adjustments so as to ensure the appropriate (necessary) equilibrium is maintained.

Insight 104:
Different forms of Price

The price paid for a good can take various forms.

a) A price paid can be the fee to effect a change of property, in that the ownership of the good is transferred to whoever pays the price from whoever receives the price.

b) A price paid can be the fee to affect the use of a good without effecting a charge of ownership. This form itself is divisible to two further types:-

    i.   Exclusive - in that the price paid affects a sole or exclusive right of use to the exclusion of any other potential users.

    ii.   Inclusive - in that the price affects an inclusive use, potentially with other users sharing such use.

c) Royalties are a form of Inclusive non ownership changing Price. These can be perpetual and thus hereditary.

The Rights to non-ownership transferring Prices (rents) can themselves be considered as property that can be bought and sold for a particular Price.

Rent generating property can only exist in a state of monopolised property. This can thereby only be possible in a condition of imperfect competition, such as monopoly or oligopoly.

Insight 105:
Profits

How do we reconcile the difference between the notions of profit as:

1. The singular sum of revenue less costs.

2. The Macro perspective, as the growth of net assets.

It could reasonably be presumed that the accumulative effect of an aggregation of singular profits will result in an accumulation of funds, to affect a net accumulation of additional assets.   However, the process of capitalisation, whereby expenditure is transformed into assets, distorts this otherwise apparent identity.

Costs are no longer fully deducted from Revenue. An increasing proportion of expenditure is denominated as assets (Assetification). The result of this is twofold:

a) Costs are reduced whilst revenue is otherwise unaltered, so as to increase singular profits.

b) Macro profits are also increased by the growth in assets.

There also seems to be an alignment here with the Kaleckian adage that "Capitalists earn what they spend".

Insight 106:
Inequality

Inequality, whether it be wealth or health, has negative impact upon the vast majority in society. Both have social costs that have to been borne by all. Although some bear those costs as a necessary price paid to be at the advantageous end of the equality continuum.

Nevertheless, for the majority upon that continuum, that price tends to reduce as disparities of inequality diminishes. This, of course, is a theoretical claim rather than a universal and unequivocally proven fact. Those at the *positive* end of the spectrum will have an interest in disputing such a claim; not least in demanding indisputable proof of its validity.

Some, however, might view it as a normative position. Others might point out that the costs of inequality are only measurable (and even conceivable) in a situation where it has been greatly reduced.

The push away from the normative towards the positive (i.e. scientific and thus measurable) inevitably favours those being favoured by inequality

The use of mathematical analysis on social actions is mistaken. Random acts may create apparently patterned events. Although we may know how the pattern appears, its causation is not systematic, only random, and we cannot determine its cause.

This is just a repeat of the *deductive error*.

These fallacies are exaggerated when dealing with human choice that make otherwise inanimate elements follow apparent patterns, but those choices are conceived as largely unaffected by those patterns.

For example, the Sun is unaffected by the fact that it rises earlier each day for half the year. It is of no consequence to the Sun that after midsummer's night it rises later rather than earlier. By contrast human action is not impartial. Human choices and interaction are consequently reactive and contextually contingent.

Being able to predict is undoubtedly useful, but is not deterministic science. Correlation is not causation; predictability is not knowledge; high probability is not certainty.

Our conceptions are based on our theoretical underpinnings of our perceptions. The biases inbuilt to our perceptions are borne out in our conceptions. They become an almost self-serving and self-fulfilling prophesy. This may be fine for most practical purposes, but are intrinsically flawed. These flaws inevitably lead to such events as the relatively recent financial crash and crises.

The proliferation of the advocation and use of *Big Data* should be seen as the exploitation of the methodological illiterate or at best naive, to salvage mathematical usage as a predictive tool. Perhaps, in the interests of those practiced in the use of such tools, and those producing those tools and products (such as Bloomberg, Microsoft and IBM).

Insight 107:
Wealth

Wealth is the ability to use and consume goods and services. Differentiated wealth, the form preferred by those with most wealth, requires an unequal distribution of these ability levels.

This inequality is required by the wealthier classes so as to ensure the relative superiority of their position.

With changes within an economy, relative wealth, rather than absolute wealth, is deemed as the most important factor; particularly by those with the largest proportions of that wealth. As wealth generates power, these most powerful wealth holders are able to wield the most power, and thereby influence.

Insight 108:
Distribution and Auctions

Introduction to Auctions:- what are the problems that Auctions are intended and designed to resolve?

1. What is the appropriate value of an item (as quantified by Price) at any particular moment?

2. How do we distribute items most effectively? (i.e. to those with the highest valuations, given that higher valuations equate to higher utility.)

These are fundamentally the prime problems of Neoclassical Economics. These can and should be contrasted with the main problem of Classical Political Economy - how do we produce more goods more productively?

Insight 109:
Rent is Theft.

I saw some graffiti on a shop window one morning that said "Rent is theft". As rent in economic terms is "unearned income" this slogan must effectively be accurate.

If employment is equivalent to renting one's Labour to your employer, is the Labourer robbed or are they robbing the Capitalist? Where does the robbery reside within Human Rental relationships?

For economists such as J.B. Clark and David Ellerman, it is the Labourers that are being robbed. This is due to the direction of the power [i.e. Capital] relationships affecting t (rent).

Wages (w) are effectively a negative form of rent, whereby:

$$w < z^L$$

(where z^L is a productivity coefficient of Labour)

Insight 110:
Rent

Absolute Rent [t^A] equates to unearned income, whereas *Differential Rent* [t^D] (so-called Ricardian Rent) is proportional to productivity [*mp*].

When wages are greater than marginal productivity [$w > mp$], then *Absolute Rent* is being earned by the Labourer in excess of their Differential Rent (*mp*).

When wages are less than marginal productivity [$w < mp$], surplus value is being extracted from Labour. Some of this surplus value will be the Labourers' *Differential Rent* (t^D as mp), but some may also be constituted by *Absolute Rent*.

When wages are equal to the labourers' marginal productivity [$w = mp$] only Differential Rent is being extracted by the Labourer (no *Absolute Rent*). Although *Absolute Rent* may still be being extracted, it is all accumulated by the Capitalist who is paying for the Labour.

However!
Should rent be solely the *Differential Rent* (mp) given that *mp* is always less than the average productivity overall (if we accept diminishing *mp*) or perhaps even absolute. If wages are only equal to the *mp* rather than average productivity [*ap*], then the Labourer's remuneration will always be less than their productivity.

Capitalists have a power to curtail wages to *mp* rather than *ap*. Profits include this differential [$ap - mp$], as a component of exploitation.

If production occurred at the point of maximum productivity then profits would be at their zenith. However, if production occurs at a point less than maximum rate of profits, i.e. at mp, then profits will not be at their maximum rate even if that are at the maximum amount.

Marginalism recommends production of the maximum amount rather than maximum rate of profit. By doing so wages and profits are both curtailed.

Capitalism pursues the maximum rate of profit whilst giving lip-service to a notional maximum amount, so as to attempt to maximise profits even greater by diminishing wages with the fallacy that they must equate to the mp (i.e. $< ap$).

Insight 111:
Ricardo's Notion of Rent

Introduction

The prime objection within this *insight* to Ricardo's notion of rent stems from the idea that rent is due from differences in fertility or what Ricardo referred to as "the original and indestructible powers of the soil" (Ricardo, I, p.67) in both different qualities and quantities of land.

What is normally meant by fertility is the productivity of a piece of land, which is then usually viewed in relation with the size of the plot. If one acre of land can produce 100 kilos of corn and another acre 200 kilos of corn, then the latter is viewed as twice as fertile as the first. There is, perhaps. apparently little that could be quibbled with on this. However, this is a very superficial account and as such does not portray the true intricacies of the question of fertility.

Return on units of labour (and capital)

Ricardo recognised that it is the return from land in relation to the labour and capital used on that land which should be the measure of its productivity.

> for rent is always the difference between the produce obtained by the employment of two equal quantities of capital and labour.[28] (ibid, p.71)

Ricardo perceived capital as little more than labour in another form. So as to alleviate problems of

---

[28] There is a *problem* here with the issue of the quantification of Capital and for that matter labour. Which is why, perhaps, Ricardo stuck with an exclusively corn model.

complication we (like Ricardo) can initially look at examples using only nominal quantities of labour.

So, in our simple case mentioned above, we could take the first acre of land as only producing 100 kilos of corn and requiring one man working 1000 hours over the season. If the second acre of land produces the 200 kilos, also with 1000 man-hours then this second obviously has greater fertility than the first plot does.

However, if we drop the assumption that the two portions of land are the same acreage then different issues arise. Ricardo, in his chapter on rent in On the *Principles of Political Economy and Taxation* (1821), makes only a few remarks regarding the size or quantity of land used in agriculture, he relates generally to portions of land. If the assumption is that the portions must be the same then I aim to show that this assumption is dubious.

To continue our example, one acre with 1000 man-hours will produce 100 kilos of corn, but the second plot is two acres, which with 1000 man-hours will produce 200 kilos of corn; or to summarise;

Case I

Land A -	1 acre + 1000 hrs	= 100 kilos
Land B -	2 acres + 1000 hrs	= 200 kilos
or	1 acre + 500 hrs	= 100 kilos

This shows that an acre of the second land is twice as productive as the first portion. One thing this example shows us is the need to differentiate between productivity and fertility. *Fertility* then is the quality that relates land to its output potential, independent of the amount of labour or capital to gain that level. In the case above both types of land have the same fertility, as they can produce the same output per acre.

However, productivity is probably more of interest to a farmer, they would prefer the productivity of land B, as they would have to work only half as much. Or to put it another way the cost of production of corn on B is half that as on A. As Ricardo would stipulate rent would then be due on land B, given that the market price would be determined by the cost of production on land A (which would bear no rent).

Thus, in simple terms the cost of corn would equate to the 10 hrs per kilo required to produce it on land A. However, the farmer on land B is producing corn at a relative "price" (cost) of 5 hrs per kilo. Given that there must be equal rates of profit to the farmers there must be rent due to equalise both farmers' (lands') returns.

Let us assume the standard rate of profit is 10%. Then the price of corn from land A will equate to 11 hrs per kilo. If this is the acceptable market price, then land A will return the equivalent of 1100 hrs for the 1000 hours expended. Thus, land B should return 1100 hrs for the 1000 hour expended. However, at a "price" of corn (at 11 hrs per kilo) it would return 2200 hrs for the 1000 hours expended..

Land B has thus produced a surplus (above the "normal") equivalent to 1100 hrs that must (according to Ricardo's theory) be paid as rent to the landlord at a rate of 550 hrs per acre. So, although the fertility (as we have qualified it above) is the same on both lands, the difference in productivity has given rise to the rent.

If we change our example such that the plot of land referred to as land A is now also two acres, thus

Case II

Land A -	2 acre + 1000 hrs	= 100 kilos
or	1 acre + 500 hrs	= 50 kilos
Land B -	2 acres + 1000 hrs	= 200 kilos
or	1 acre + 500 hrs	= 100 kilos

Thus, it is obvious that both the fertility and the productivity of land B is superior. So, taking land A as the price determining (with 10% profit) the price is still 11 hrs per kilo, and likewise the costs on land B have not changed and hence the rent level is as in Case *I*. This seems to show that what would commonly be known as fertility has paid no part in determining rent, but emphasises that it is the productivity of land in relation to labour that is the true determinant.

If we continue the example further to extend the size of land B thus

Case III

Land A	1 acre + 1000 hrs	= 100 kilos
Land B	5 acres + 1000 hrs	= 200 kilos
or	1 acre + 200 hrs	= 40 kilos

Thus, the fertility of land A is superior to land B's (per acre), but the profitability of using the five acres instead of one is evident in its productivity or the reward to the same amount of labour used.

It may be argued that it could not be the case that five acres and one acre could be farmed with the same amount of labour and produce the same output, or even a greater output (in the least fertile). However, if we look at the situation acre by acre, we can see that the real assumption is only that although land A can produce two and a half as much output as land B it requires five times as much labour so to do. Or to put another way all that is required is that there are no fixed coefficients of production.

However, in Case III equal quantities of labour are used, but on different volumes of land to produce different levels of output. If we drop the quantitative specification on the land component, then we would get;

Plot A + 1000 hrs   = 100 kilos

Plot B + 1000 hrs   = 200 kilos

This reflects what Ricardo reproduces in his chapter on rent. With the result that rent is due on plot B because of its extra fertility. This is the comparative fertility of plots, without reference to acreage.

Example from Ricardo — Page 67
Ricardo noted in his opening remarks defining rent that if there were "two adjoining farms of the same extent, and of the same natural fertility", one of which has the benefits of farm buildings and agricultural man-made advantages (e.g. ditches) then the developed farm would command an extra fee (as profit on the labour used to implement the changes) above the true rent due for the "original and indestructible powers of the soil" (Ricardo, 1821, p.67). If the word "extent" is taken to mean size then this can be seen as just an emphasis on his example. To assume this one utterance is then implied un-stated throughout the rest of the work is ungrounded.

Example from Ricardo — Page 68
When considering forests and mines, and comparing the payments made as true rent with other payments

made just for the crops that happen to be positioned upon the land (trees or coal), he noted of the former;

> such compensation might justly be called rent, because it is paid for the productive powers of the land (Ricardo, 1821, p.68).

This reference is to the productive powers; there is no mention of quantity or amount of land used.

Examples from Ricardo — Page 69
Ricardo noted that "On the first settling of a country" land is used like air or water when freely available. Thus such "gifts of nature" are employed in "incessant use", because they are "inexhaustible" and their "supply is boundless" (Ricardo, 1821, p.69).

Thus, the use of land would be made without reference to quantity. If land is available without limit then the farmers' only consideration will be the amount of work (labour & capital) necessary to produce the maximum crop. Consideration to the amount of a resource utilised is only an issue when there is a perceived finite supply. If air is viewed as being without limit in supply, then there is no consideration to how much is used, in fact it is seen as an irrelevant question. As such the quantity of land would be an irrelevant question (at the first settling of a country) if it is available endlessly. Thus, Ricardo cannot and does not refer to plot size at this stage.

Examples from Ricardo — Page 70
Ricardo then noted that if all land had the same qualities, and was unlimitedly available then "no charge could be made for its use". However, "land is not unlimited in quantity and uniform in quality", and hence "land of an inferior quality" has to be brought into

production. This progression carries on as increasingly less fertile lands are utilised. However, if the quantity of land cannot be taken as an issue (as for p.69 above) then only the quality can be of import. Ricardo makes no such claim (Ricardo, 1821, p.70).

Examples from Ricardo — Page 71
When specifying that rent may arise by the use of extra capital being "employed on the old land" more profitably then on new (lesser fertile) land, he noted:

> rent is always the difference between the produce obtained by the employment of two equal quantities of capital and labour (Ricardo 1821, p.71)

There is no mention of the relation to the size of plots involved.

Examples from Ricardo — Page 72
Ricardo noted that a landlord can only increase rents in line with new productivity levels "at the expiration of his lease". Thus, rent is due per leasehold, there is no mention of rent due per acreage. In practical terms a farm may not have uniform fertility throughout its range and hence rent would be due to its productivity as a whole rather than by field or acre. Hence again Ricardo cannot and does not mention acreage (Ricardo, 1821, p.72).

Examples from Ricardo — Page 74
Ricardo made the comment that "more labour is required on the inferior lands" (Ricardo, 1821, p.74). This should be taken to mean than to produce the same output on the superior lands. Hence again there is no mention of land's quantity only of its productive power in relation to applied labour, whether capital or direct labour.

The value of corn is regulated by the quantity of labour bestowed on its production on that quality of land, or with that portion of capital, which pays no rent. (Ricardo, 1821, p.74).

Hence the value of corn is not regulated by the quantity of land required for its production. From this passage it might even be judged that the quality of land bestows nothing towards the value of corn.

Examples from Ricardo — Page 77

But that corn which is produced by the greatest quantity of labour is the regulator of the price of corn (Ricardo, 1821, p.77).

If the quantity of labour is the regulator of price, then not only is the fertility, but also the quantity of land, irrelevant to the price of corn. There seems to be a strange assertion in Ricardo's notion of rent in that if rent levels are determined by fertility and rent does not enter into the determination of price, then fertility plays no part in determining price. This is obviously not the case for as Ricardo acknowledges changes in land's fertility may affect price.

Examples from Ricardo — Page 79

With the discussion of agricultural improvements causing the need to discontinue the use of land of the "third" fertility, there is still no mention of the quantity of land. There is not even a reference to less land being used. It is only noted that "the capital and labour employed on No. 3 will be devoted to the production of other commodities". This alleviates the position of land being left idle.

The next paragraph qualifies what is meant by agricultural improvements. They are not direct increases in land's fertility but "rather in consequence of less labour being bestowed on its production". Thus agricultural improvements are producing the same output using less labour (Ricardo, 1821, p.79).

Thus, if a new technique required more actual land in production, but less labour then this would be an improvement that would or could lower price. Such a technique could be the use of cordons for fruit production rather than trees. Cordons take up more physical space then trees but require less labour and are even conducive to the use of labour saving machines. Thus, showing that the quantity of land is an irrelevancy to productivity.

Examples from Ricardo — Page 80
Ricardo identified two types of agricultural improvements

1) Improvements that "enable us to produce the same produce from a smaller quantity of land". This would be of the kind "which increase the productive powers of the land".

2) The other improvements "enable us, by improving our machinery, to obtain its produce with less labour". This would be using the same quantity of land but with less labour.

Ricardo pointed out that these are only improvements if they "lead to a fall in price". This must be so "for it is the essential quality of an improvement to diminish the quantity of labour before required to produce a commodity". Thus, this proviso must be appended to the first type of improvement - the use of a less quantity of both land and labour (Ricardo, 1821, p.80).

Thus, we have two types of improvements, both of which must require less labour to produce the same output as previously. However, this may be with the same or less quantity of land as before the improvement. But as was noted above it is possible for a new technique to require less labour, but a greater quantity of land. This is especially the case when the introduction of machines in agriculture offset savings in manpower against a need for the use of more land.

Ricardo assumes that a change "which will enable me to make a piece of land produce 20 per cent. more corn" will necessarily allow the withdrawal of "at least a portion of my capital" (Ricardo, 1821, p.80). It must do or else it fails his own definition of an agricultural improvement.

One problem Ricardo has is that by defining rent as due to the "original and indestructible power of the soil" he cannot make allowances for changes in the ranking of the fertility of land. His examples have land of first, second, third, etc. qualities and that changes in technology can alleviate the need for the use of the lowest type with rent then being the difference in productivity between the first and last used. His system can make no allowance for changes in his ranking of lands' fertility. A technical change may reduce the otherwise superior to a lower ranking, with all the confusing rental changes that would imply.

Examples from Ricardo — Page 82

But there are improvements which may lower the relative value of produce without lowering the corn rent, though they will lower the money rent of land. Such improvements do not increase the productive powers of the land; but they enable us to obtain its produce for less labour. (Ricardo, 1821, p.82).

Here Ricardo is attempting perhaps to deal with the situation put forward above where "Less capital, which is the same thing as less labour, will be employed on the land; but to obtain the same produce, less land cannot be cultivate." (Ricardo, 1821, p.82). Hence, Ricardo asked the question as to whether such changes actually diminish rents. To answer this, he gave two examples.

The first in which four portions of capital are employed "each giving the same results". Improvements in technology enable all four portions of capital to be reduced by the same amount (i.e. 50, 60, 70 and 80 become 45, 55, 65 and 75). In this case although the nominal rent may fall, the real (or corn) rent will be unchanged, as there is no difference between 80 less 50 and 75 less 45.

The other case assumes that the improvement is such that the less productive capital's use can be negated by the continued use of the others at their new productivity. This would mean that initially each portion of capital produced 100 units of output, but after the change each of the three remaining lots of land, using the same labour and land, would have to produce 133⅓ (100 X 4 divided by 3) units of output.

However, this cannot be to Ricardo's intentions as if this were the case then the productivity of the least productive capital would have improved more than the formerly superior capital. In the case above now both the 50 and the 70 units are now producing 133⅓ units whereas before they were producing only 100. Thus the 50 was originally producing a surplus of 50 units, which has increased to 83⅓ units. However, the surplus of the 70 units of capital has more than doubled from 30 to 63⅓ - this would be incompatible with an idea of diminishing returns.

However, Ricardo specified that this model is supposed to have the same amount of land in use as previously, so it must be assumed that the four original plots are still in use but only with the sum of the first three amounts of capital.

If the original capital on the four plots were reduced by 20 units, this would then be the same combined amount as originally used on the three most fertile plots. This gives a new capital distribution of 30, 40, 50, and 60: which is a problem as this represents the original difference of capital of 30, ([60 — 30] = [75 — 45] = [80 - 50]), for the production of equal degrees of output. Thus; Ricardo's statement "corn rent would immediately fall" (Ricardo, 1821, p.83) would not necessarily be true, for as he stated,

> because the difference between the capital most productive, and the capital least productive would [but not in this case] be diminished; and it is this difference which constitutes rent (Ricardo, 1821, p.83).

The only way in which the re-allocation of the first three portions of capital could be done evenly and reducing rent would be for a change in productivity as a proportion of the original requirements. In this case a reduction to approximately 69.23% of the original capital to produce 34.6 41.5 48.5, and 55.4 (rounded to single decimal positions). Thus, causing an immediate fall in rent to 20.8.

However, such an even change in these effects would not fit with the dictates of the notion of diminishing returns with the new technology. Which may be why originally, he used the example of a straight reduction of five units on each capital lot as this represents diminishing returns.

Competitive effects

If rent ensures that all profits are equalised through its mechanisms, then there is no incentive for a farmer to use one piece of land in contrast to another. For his return can only be subject to the same maximum. Thus, there is no motive for the use of the more fertile or even productive lands first, for by paying less rent his profit will still be fixed by the market.

The difficulty of quantifying quantity

If productivity were still insisted upon as related to the acreage of land one could initially ask whether it was the actual surface area of land or the area as presented on a map that was the defining character.

If it is the actual physical area of land surface that is the measure then such schemes that alter the surface area would then affect the relative fertility without altering the "original and indestructible powers of the soil". However, terracing would be an expenditure of capital and labour that affected land's output and thus altered the capital employed to output ratio, but also altered the acreage, with indeterminate results. Likewise, if map acreage, which is thus of fixed specification, can have its output changed by alteration of the physical surface therein, then indeterminate effects can be envisaged.

Variability of soils

McVickar noted that "The poorest lands are always let in immense tracts" (McVickar, 1825, p.122), due to the fact that the bulk of these lands are infertile and would thus carry no rent. He pointed out that rent was hence not due to the fertility of whole tracts, but only for those parts therein that are "the more fertile spots intermixed with them" (McVickar, 1825, p.123). Thus, rent was a result of the overall fertility of an expanse of land and not any portion or specific area within it.

Other issues:

- If rent increases as productivity decreases; then rent decreases as productivity increases.

- Therefore, the interests of those benefitting from rent is to sabotage productivity – i.e. conserve the current technology = conservatism.

- Or to increase demand greater than the rate of productivity can increase.

- Is a change in productivity - a change in the K/L ratio or a change in the input/output ratio?

- If "rent is always the difference between the produce obtained by the employment of two equal quantities of capital and labour." (Ricardo, 1821, p.71): then given there was no mention of land here, why is equality of plot size assumed?

- Two equal quantities of K & L thus result is two different quantities of rent (t).

- These two different quantities of rent (t) must be due to a difference in quantity in some other factor. In a model where it is assumed that there are just the three factors (Capital, Labour, and Land), this other factor must be land. The quantity is obviously not of issue, so it must be the productivity of a plot, rather than its quantity.

- Rent (as an output) is proportional or relative to the quantity of the Capital and Labour inputs, but not to the quantity of Land (considered as an input). As such, how can rent be due to the productivity of the Land input? Surely, it must be relevant to the other inputs (K and L)?

- However, perhaps all the inputs should be viewed as qualities rather than quantities?

- In a like manner, Thomas Hodgskin in *Labour Defended* (1825) illustrated that it is not the quantity but the quality of Capital that is of issue.

- Likewise, Smith and Marx both had issues with the quantity of Labour and highlight the issues are relevant to the quality.

- There is by this means an issue such that, how do we (if at all possible) quantify productivity or quality? Generally, it, particularly the former, is conceived in relation to the nominal quantities of inputs and outputs.

- However, if these other inputs themselves are not quantifiable, how is it possible to quantify the rent derived from them?

- A solution is then to consider only the nominal quantities involved (i.e. the nominal prices paid for them). However, Ricardo was critical of Smith for apparently doing this.

Insight 112:
Pseudo Markets

Pseudo Markets are a part of business strategies or arrangements (such as gambling) that are intended to have the appearance of, and promulgated as, market exchanges. However, they are not in fact economically fair (or equitable) exchanges. They are implicitly deceptive and exploitative.

Insight 113:
Fetishisms

Fetishisms (in the Marxist sense) in Economics are the results of distorted value judgements. Goods are valued far above any *realistic* or otherwise *justifiable* value.

This can be the result of advertising, fashion, or socialised peer pressure.

Or, quite often, asymmetric information, which initiates consumer ignorance. Over confidence can also result from informational failings, and create fashionable fetishism.

An alternative view is that as values are nothing intrinsic, but are purely idiosyncratically and subjective, there can be no incorrect valuations, and hence no fetishism.

If there can be no incorrect valuations, it can therefore be argued that not only are fetishisms impossible, but also exploitation is out of the question.

Insight 114:
Prices and the Quantity Theory of Money (QTM)

Normally it is seen that if the amount of money in an economy increases, *ceteris paribus* (i.e. everything else remaining the same), then the Prices in that system will increase accordingly.

If, however, that economy's productivity increases at the same rate as the money supply then Prices can be left unchanged. If productivity gains are sufficiently large, so as to exceed the increase in the money supply, or if there is no change to the money supply, then Prices may be decreased.

However, if money supply increases facilitate a larger proportional increase in the velocity of money, then Prices will fall, if the QTM holds true.

As such greater efficiency in the use (spending) of money will result in welfare gains as Prices decrease. Likewise, a reduction in the velocity of money, for example, caused by saving, will lead to price rises.

The velocity of money, as a measure of its flow, essentially changes the amount of money within an economy. As such money needs to be understood as a flow (i.e. a process) rather than a stock.

Austerity, in the sense of the paying off of debts, reduces the money supply and can thereby reduce prices. Although if nominal prices are sticky and effectively unchanged, then profits will increase.

Nevertheless, if such negative money supply affects are accompanied by reduced production (i.e. less goods) in an economy, then prices may be forced to rise and/or profits to decrease. Although if profits remain unchanged then real wages will be negatively affected.

If price decreases result in deferred spending, then price increases should result in accelerated spending, and saving will diminish. Reduced saving will in turn increase production, which, with a constant money supply will subsequently reduce prices.

Simplistic Effects of Money Supply Changes

MS change	Money	Orig. goods	Prod. Change	New output	prices	Change
	£100	100			£1.00	
10%	£110	100			£1.10	10.0%
-10%	£90	100			£0.90	-10.0%
10%	£110	100	10%	110	£1.00	0.0%
10%	£110	100	8%	108	£1.02	1.9%
10%	£110	100	12%	112	£0.98	-1.8%
-10%	£90	100	-10%	90	£1.00	0.0%
-10%	£90	100	-8%	92	£0.98	-2.2%
-10%	£90	100	-12%	88	£1.02	2.3%

Section 8
Production

Insight 115:
Production

Production is a function in the sense that it is a process. As such its component parts (capital, Labour and land) are also processes. For production to be considered rather as a mathematical function is, at best, to misunderstand the very nature of production.

Production as a process is the resultant culmination of its component contributing elements - that are each, in their own rights, processes. As such it is an ensuing flux wherein its elements are themselves constituted series of fluxes. If we are to understand their impact upon humanity and humanity's role in its continuation, production needs to be understood from a predominately praxiological perspective.

The attempts to quantify the elements of production are vain attempts to quantify production itself in order to conceive production as a mathematical function. Thereby they are effectively rhetorical devices to justify its outcomes' distribution to interested and vested parties.

In its concrete reality, Production's outcomes are just as incapable of quantification as its inputs.

Insight 116:
Production Functions

An economic production function is an attempt to represent a complex temporal series of events as an oversimplification of relationships in terms of the likewise oversimplified notions of relatively arbitrary factors of production. These factors are commonly presented as Capital, Labour and Land, and are generally conceived as physical entities that are quantifiable, finite and efficacious.

These factors are incoherent in real terms and should be accepted as abstractions. As such the quantitative assignments allotted them must likewise be conceived as unreal abstractions. Thus, any attempt to use these abstract measurements for meaningful purposes, must be recognized as both woefully inadequate and wildly inaccurate as representatives of the original processes that form what economists call, or mean by, *Production*.

Despite its necessarily fictional nature, this formalization of productive processes mutates from a retrospective abstraction not only to an accounting identity, but to a predictive tool. It becomes easier to follow this formulaic fiction than to deal with the multifaceted realities of such creative and fluid processes. The freeform creative processes are mutated into rigid procedures.

Such diversification can also be seen in other creative processes - for example, political social production in the guise of economic policy. These now are built and promulgated in terms of the interests of factor defined class interests and calculated almost exclusively with regards to these fictional elements.

This original abstract and thereby unreal method of observation has grown into an unquestionable tool and methods. It is almost as if a doctor simplified their understanding of the human body into four or five static key factors and then proceeded to medicate all ills solely in relation to these few entities. Thereby foregoing any considerations of the relationships between these factors and all other internal and importantly external factors, as well as all dynamic issues and the inherent flux, evolution and aging of the human form.

Insight 117:
Four Theories of the Cause of Production

There are as, Aristotle said, four ways of looking at causes. This is reflected in Economics in the different ways we have to understand production:

a) The efficient cause perspective adopts a *Labour Theory of Production* such that Labour is the effective cause of all goods (and thereby value).

b) The material cause view cites Sraffa's *The Production of Commodities by Means of Commodities* as the determinant factor.

c) A formal cause understanding would perhaps utilize the circuitist's *Monetary Theory of Production*. The power subsequent to a monetary system's structure being the crucial factor.

d) The final cause theorist would stick to the neoclassical subjectivity conception of demand-determined production.

In reality production is likely to be resultant from an ever-varying combinations of two or more (if not all) of these factors.

Whichever is dominant (whether actual, or just treated or conceive as) is likely to be the consequent of political machinations. Thus, economics must be political and subordinate to subjective arguments, opinion and debate.

Insight 118:
Production as a
Keynesian *Beauty Contest*

When production is private, in the sense of being decentralised, production decisions are up to individuals left to face the discipline of the Market.

Do they produce to meet their own needs? No, they produce to meet the needs of the wider population – i.e. to meet the needs of all their potential consumers.

Or do they? Do they produce to address the requirements of what distributers think the consumers need?

Or do they? Do they produce to address the requirements of what marketeers think the consumers need?

Or do they produce to meet the needs of what wholesalers think the consumers need?

Or do they produce to meet the needs of what retailers think the consumers need?

Which iteration? Will it be the same for all goods, all markets, all areas?

Insight 119:
Production's Purpose.

Production was initially concerned with the creation of commodities.[29]   However, with the development of capitalism, *production* (in the sense of business activity) is now primarily concerned with the creation of addition capital - i.e. the accumulation of capital.   Given that capital is distinguished from the commodities (in terms of its end destination), it is inevitable that there must be some compromise or conflict of interest in terms of the end product.

The modern focus of Capitalism, particularly in its present-day guise of Financialisation, is increasingly focused upon the reproduction and accumulation of financial (as opposed to physical) capital.

From this perspective, Industry is concerned with the production of commodities (i.e. wealth), whereas Business is preoccupied with the production of Profits (principally defined as the increase of Capital Assets). This conflict between the two, equates to Economic Sabotage.

As von Mises said, production has to take into account the needs not only of the producers but also their customers. However, the crucial decision made by the Capitalist is the assignment of output between consumption goods and reproductive goods (as capital goods or as Austrian Economists called them, Goods of

---

[29] By Commodities we mean goods and services produced, not for the producers' consumption, but rather produced with the intention of trading them in exchange for some form of remuneration.

Higher Order). Austrians thereby see the Capitalists' Output Decisions as being between Goods of First (or Lower) Order, and varying degrees of Goods of Higher Order.

The Post Keynesian position is that such decisions are made exclusively by the Capitalists, which effectively determines how much of society's output is available for consumption (i.e. Real Wages) and how much is allocated to future capital. This decision is, Post Keynesians argue, made by capitalists with regards to their future capital profit expectations.

Alternatively, it may well be that the rate of Profit and the amount consumers are willing to spend, both impact on this decision?

If Capitalists determine how much is available to consume within an economy, then all that is so allocated will be purchased with the available stock of money. Under the application of QTM , prices are thus a function of the available money and the quantity of goods made available. This effectively means that Say's law can be said to apply as any goods produced for consumption will be consumed.

If the designated consumption goods are restricted, their price will rise according. Scarcity then becomes a necessary result of capitalists' market power. Increased imperfect competition is necessary to maintain this market power. This *Scarcity* is the direct consequence of Imperfect Competition. This effectively implies that wealth (surplus) is the consequence of Perfect Competition.

Business sabotages the economy and wealth to create profits and accumulate capital, by enforcing Imperfect Competition.

In the extreme consumption goods made available must be maintained, for some sectors of the economy, at levels below subsistence to maintain the illusion of scarcity in order to maintain high price levels and thereby Imperfect Competition.

There are different formulations of Wealth:

- **Individual Wealth:** the power possessed by an individual to consume and produce commodities.

- **Consumption Wealth:** being the social wealth of goods and services available for individual, household, and social consumption. Services include potential productive services and technology.

- **Capitalist Wealth:** being the net Capital Assets within an economy.

Consumption Wealth will tend to be greater than the sum of all Individual Wealth. In a developed capitalist economy, there may well be an inverse relationship between Capitalist Wealth and Consumption Wealth.

Insight 120:
Productivity Illusion

The concept of productivity is an illusion. As a concept it can be generalised as the ability to add value to an originally agreed value. Given that the concept of value is intrinsically subject, it cannot be quantified or even known with any known certainty.

When dealing without the incumbency of values, but the simplicity of an homogeneous output, productivity can be understood as the ability to create more of a particular good, solely by means of that good. The corn models of Classical Economists provide simple expressions of these.

An illusion is perpetrated when money, or even more fictionally, Capital, are taken or used as the homogeneous good. But given that money and capital are themselves *Categorical Errors*, this is obviously a fallacy.

At best productivity can only be understood as a historical retrospective of a specific completed production activity. At a specific time, with certain particular and effectively unique conditions, a certain combination of factors were able to produce a peculiar set of outputs.

The usual desire to quantify these heterogeneous inputs and outputs, thus condenses these factors into their monetary values. However, these themselves, particularly the outputs, are quantifiably transient. They are also exclusively subjective and historically specific.

Insight 121:
Productivity Puzzles

If £1,000 of capital applied to 2 acres of land produces a profit of £100 then the productivity relative to that land is £50 per acre.

If that £1,000 of capital applied to 4 acres of land subsequently produces a £160 surplus, then the productivity relative to that land is, seemingly, £40 an acre. This would apparently represent a decrease in productivity.

However, if we are solely concerned with the productivity of the Capital, then this (Capital's profitability) has increased from 10% to 16%.

The capitalist is only concerned with their Capital outlay, so would be content to use seemingly less productive (in per acre terms) land.

The same could be applicable to the use of Labour. For example, if (with the same £1,000 of Capital) using 20 labour hours produces £100 excess whereas using 40 labour hours produces an additional £160, then the later £4 per hour would be preferable to the apparently more productive £5 per hour.

In both these examples, Capital's productivity is inversely related to that of the other factors of production. This is not to say that this is always necessarily so, only to illustrate that Capital's productivity is not directly related to its co-factors. The Capitalist thus will not necessarily and exclusively pursue the use of the most productive factors in their pursuit of maximising profits.

It also illustrates that the productivity of land and thereby its ability to generate rent need not be directly related. The ability to generate rents seems to be more related to the productivity of the Capital used upon it, then its own inherent or indestructible powers.

Insight 122:
The Marginal Gain Illusion

The Marginal Gain Game

The possibility that a marginal gain can always be had,[30] is a prospect used to tease and tempt people to cheat (i.e. to outdo someone) or to install the fear of being cheated (i.e. being out done by somebody else). This is somewhat akin to a Prisoner's Dilemma position.

The socially optimal position, it is assumed, can always be improved upon for at least one participant, even though that advantage will inevitably come to the detriment of at least one other participant. The option then is to attempt to gain an advantage, rather than risk being taken advantage of. Thus, the socially optimal position will always be compromised, and will effectively breakdown.

A Resolution

If we aim to counter the illusion of Marginal Gain, then we need to create and support the reality of Co-operative Maximising Gain. This could be done in two (or possibly three) modes.

Firstly, by promoting the validity of Process Philosophy. This would effectively illustrate that the Marginal Gain Illusion can be understood as an example of the Fallacy of Concrete Abstraction.

Secondly, promoting the benefits of co-operative (i.e. non-marginal) production as the means to maximising social output and maximising society's rate of profit rather than merely the amount of an individual's profit.

---

[30] Possible under Cartesian Mathematics but not Newtonian.

Indeed, co-operative production is the only viable means to reverse the otherwise inevitable tendency for the rate of profit to fall. The falling rate of profit is the consequence of individualized production arrangements.

That being said, within an economy operating under conditions of Perfect Competition, the rate of profit would be reduced to zero by competitive forces. Effectively, under Perfect Competition, business profits are eliminated in favour of Consumer Surplus. In this manner the benefits of improved productivity are transferred to the consumers rather than being acquired and accumulated by private businesses.

Co-operative production, in this manner, is the inevitable consequence of Perfect Competition. When Hodgskin and Veblen discussed businesses sabotaging the economy, in effect they were pointing out that business necessarily sabotages Perfect Competition.

Thus, the improving profit rate referred to above is that social profit that necessarily increases as productivity improves, rather than the aggregate profit rate of individualized businesses.

In this way it might reasonably be argued that the promotion of Perfect Competition, as the remedy to business' sabotaging of the economy, was the third mode in countering the Marginal Gain Illusion.

Historical perspective.
Adam Smith equated improving productivity with decreasing Natural Prices. Thomas Hodgskin developed this point with his ideas of endogenous growth, which in turn furthered the concepts of Enlightenment growth and progress.

Utilitarianism should be understood as the negative reaction against this progressive Classical Political Economy.

Probability Illusions
People tend to overestimate the probability of unlikely events, but underestimate the likelihood off highly probable events. As money and power can be gained via these errors, these illusions are encouraged and perpetuated by those seeking to advantage themselves at the cost of others.

Marketing is the management of expectations in order to manipulate these illusions. Capitalism is a system that seems to incorporate these illusions to further profit a select few, whereas Socialism is a system that necessitates and requires accurate and realistic understanding of event probabilities.

Insight 123:
Pareto Optimality

Pareto Optimality creates the optimal level of output and thereby use of technology that ensures society's utility is maximised so that no one's lot could be improved without detrimental impact upon any individual. It presumes that there is a unique Goldilocks' position for this criterion.

This implies that there is a single (unique) technological combination of production factors for this Pareto Optimal output level. However, given that (at least) one of these factors of production itself has its utility level determined by this output level and its subsequent technology utilisation (i.e. the labourers' utility is related to how much labour is a part of the technological outcome), different technological combinations may result in equal utility outcomes.

Thus, the Pareto Optimal position is not necessarily unique.

Another issue is that as utility is not only unknowable, but also idiosyncratically variable, this unique position is inherently unfathomable, due to its constant variations and complexities.

Section 9
Labour & Wages

Insight 124:
True Socialism

We can opt or argue for Co-operatives as the only valid form for the firm, in that labour can own or hire capital, but that it is inappropriate (i.e. legally inconsistent) for capital to own or rent labour. We are then left with an issue as to how labour can be financed in order to acquire sufficient capital. State nationalisation can provide the solution when labour cannot be otherwise self-financing.

In this manner, Socialism is not the simple ownership of the means of production, but rather the communal or social financing of Labour's ownership of the means of production.

Does this reconcile Ellerman with J.B. Clark's ""*True Socialism*" and Kaleckian *Socialist economics*?

Is this the way to counter the increasing financialisation of the economy?

Insight 125:
The Paradox of Business and Employment

Say's Law might be said to be approximately valid, for Labour, within a system of Perfect Competition. In such a market, competitive forces will be such that wages are driven upwards and profits downwards. Thereby, labour will have the upper hand and can hold out for higher wages. Any newcomer into the labour market will be employed as employers compete with each other to maintain profits against an inevitable tendency for them to diminish.

However, within an imperfect market, the Capitalists (employers) have the upper hand, so as to maintain their profits and pushdown wages. Thus, the unemployed worker will have to settle for the lowest levels of remuneration if they are to find work.

Indeed, within Imperfect Competition the impetus is to maintain a "reserve army of the unemployed" in order to subdue wages, maintain profits, and generally sabotage the economy.

The paradox of business is that it has a vested interest in destroying the economy in that profits only exist in Imperfect Competition. To create profits businesses must ensure Imperfect Competition.

This paradox's thesis plays out such that the Labourers require business to function so as to provide gainful employment. The antithesis being that the businessperson (in the Capitalist form) must of necessity exploit those Labourers in order to create the required profits.

The synthesis (resolution) from this paradox is a business form devoid of profits. This then necessitates a reform of the business firm away from Capitalist profit maximisation, to a (Worker) Co-operative business firm formulation.

Insight 126:
Subsistence Wages

Subsistence, considered from an economic point of view, needs to be understood not so much as a living wage, but as a certain propensity to consume.

Subsistence wages should be viewed such that the propensity to consume, as a proportion of Wages, equals 100%. This results in savings equal to zero. Whoever can save must have wages greater than subsistence. Alternatively, expressed, whoever does not save, must be in receipt of subsistence wages.

Whatever causes savings to equal zero, whether lowness of wages or excessiveness of expenditure, is extraneous. The causes of expenditures may be peer or social pressures. As Ricardo noted, socially necessary (or acceptability) may reduce all labourers' wages to what amounts to subsistence levels.

A paraphrasing of Parkinson's Law might be appropriate here, such that expenditure expands to meet the income available. This being the case there is no scope for savings and income must equate to subsistence wages.

Indeed, if expenditure has to be funded via borrowing (loans) then wages are less than sufficient for subsistence.

Insight 127:
Austerity and Wages

If one believes the Iron Law of Wages, then workers' wages will be held, by competition, down to a socially necessary subsistence level.

Thereby, wages have an inverse relationship with profits. Or alternatively expressed, Profits equate to the residual remaining after wages and rent have been paid out of the revenue received for goods sold.

Thereby, Austerity, by lowering the socially acceptable subsistence level, will have the effect of raising profits.

Austerity thus becomes a means to counteract the tendency for the rate of profits to fall, and thus a necessary policy for conservative economics.

Insight 128:
Monopsony Wages

When Joan Robinson and other Post-Keynesian talked about monopsony, they were effectively representing the Austrian Economics distinction between Goods of the First Order (i.e. Consumption goods), and Goods of Higher Orders (e.g. Capital, Production Goods and raw materials.

Both Austrians and Post-Keynesians acknowledge that this distinction is made by capitalists.

When made outside of Perfect Competition workers and society as a whole come off worse and Crony Capitalism sabotages the economy, as capitalists have the power to determine Labour's real wages, irrespective of nominal wage bargaining.

_____

_____

Section 10
Power

Insight 129:
Two Forms of Power.

There are two forms of power.

The first is static power, borne of the control of static entities. This power over things manifests itself primarily in the power derived from the control of ownership of property.

The second form in which power can persist is dynamic, in that it is manifest in the controls and rights over processes.

When static power, as the exclusive control of things seems to sustain those things in order to safeguard and maintain that power, it acts contrary to dynamic power. As all things are emergent, contextual and transient, any attempt to maintain and preserve static conditions will inevitability be contrary and thereby detrimental to the dynamic nature of reality.

Herein lies a fundamental paradox of production, business and wealth. To use Veblen's terms business tends to sabotage industry when we consider business as the static and industry as the dynamic.

When business is considered as the pursuit of individualistic gain of wealth in the form of static things (and power), then, in this perspective, it will be detrimental to industry, when that is considered as the dynamic advancement of social well-being.

It is a basic fallacy of composition to presume that the accumulation of static wealth will automatically equate to improved dynamic economic growth. To an extent, this is acknowledged in Keynes's "paradox of Thrift" and "Money Illusion" concepts.

The solidification or commodification of processes into vendible entities detracts (rather than adds to) the efficiency and potency of those processes. Using a river analogy - removing water from a river lessens its flow.

Keeping to this river analogy, we could allude to another fundamental issue in terms of property issues. The idea that someone owns a river in terms of the whole range of the dynamic issues inherent in the oversimplification of our concepts of a river, are generally "resolved" in terms of static solutions. Such as who owns which stretch of land through which it flows, and rights over drawing off water from its flow. As such, the inalienable nature of the river as a series of processes is lost and unconsidered.

Economics persists in its attempts to resolve dynamic complications by adopting static property rights solutions, such as Carbon Trading.

Insight 130:
Wealth and Power

One is wealthy as one has the power to increase and improve one's lot.

Alternatively, an agent might conceive their wealthiness as they improve their lot proportionally to their contemporaries. If one is increasing one's lot, but at a slower rate than one's contemporaries, then although one is better off, one might still feel a little discombobulated or aggrieved.

Thereby there could be a focus on the differential accumulation of power rather than absolute power. As such, although one's absolute power is lessened, but one is better off relatively to one's contemporaries, then one might well be happier, utility wise.

Personal utility is possibly more influenced by relative wealth than by absolute wealth. Perhaps it is simply that personal utility is easier recognized relatively than absolute. If all we can sense is motion, then relative wealth is perhaps easier conceived than absolute.

Akin to money illusion this might effectively amount to wealth illusion. Alternatively, this may simple be a consequence of our developed social existence. Might this be the necessary result of socially evolution or a result of randomized Darwinian evolution? Or simply the result of the need for reciprocal recognition from our social peers.

Insight 131:
Gold as Power

Gold itself is of very little intrinsic use. Indeed, its worth diminishes as its quantity increases. Its worth is borne of it being a flow rather than a stock. The power to control that flow amounts to a power over its value and hence embodies the exercise of power. The ability to control flows, to control supply, indeed to sabotage supply, is the essence and exercise of economic power.

The control of flows embodies differential enhanced wealth (as power).

The so-called "Law of Supply and Demand" is thereby the main weapon of power. One could question whether the attempt to control population growth is an exercise to sabotage the flow of Labour and hence the subsequent flow of all goods.

Power comes from squeezing the supply of goods, by creating unnecessary scarcity, by sabotaging the otherwise abundancy of Labour (and nature). The strangulation of output is the fount of power, and its continued expansive perpetuation.

Productive creativity is power's nemesis. Destructive innovation its ally.

Insight 132:
The Isocratic Relationship

An Isocratic Relationship is one without any asymmetric power distributions. From the Greek isos [equal] and kratos [strength] - isokratia [equality of power].

The inequalities of power within the firm generally originate with social inequalities of the distribution of Capital. Although, if we adhere to the Capital as Power notions, this explanatory expression becomes little more than a tautology.

A more positive definition of the Isocratic Firm thus needs to express the positive consequences borne from equality of power within the human constituents of the firm. These human constituents being the workers, management and owners of the firm. However, given that these three categories are primarily differentiated in terms of their relative power, there is a certain inconsistency here too.

Thus, if there is equality of distributed power, we are likely to, at the very least, weaken the borders and distinctions between the constituent partners in the firm. This is not necessarily to presume that that there will be a subsequent equality of outcomes within an Isocratic Firm.

When J.B. Clark instigated his idea of marginal productivity, it was as a test to determine whether the worker was "robbed" at the place of production. By this he meant to identify whether the Labourer received the whole of their due - the whole of their product.

His conclusion was that the Labourer did not receive their entire product. Indeed, the only situation that this could be the case would be within an economy of Perfect Competition. Perfect Competition is effectively only possible in Isocratic conditions. The path to Perfect Competition thus begins with the Isocratic Firm.

Insight 133:
Can Value be Isocratic?

Value may be determined subjectively, but nevertheless the assignment of value is the exercise of power and privilege. Especially when exercised in cases other than retrospectively, but even then, it is most often still the case.

If value is to be Isocratic, is would need to be allotted arbitrary, almost objectively. Otherwise, it (value) is inevitably undemocratic. How can a society be just when its values are the consequence of privileged power? Those that hold such power need to exercise such control to maintain their hierarchical endowments' position in the self-aggrandizement and self-preservation of their value.

To do this whilst maintaining an illusion of democratic subjective communal objectively is surely one of the greatest tricks played upon humanity. It may be this that accounts for both political and economic obedience.

Perpetration of this myth is furthered by the illusion of the Walrasian Auctioneer as an apparent arbiter of fair and appropriate Prices. As even the tyro in Auction Theory is aware, the fundamental condition for successful auctions is a monopolistic position on the part of the seller. Prices within an auction scenario are thus skewed in favour of the seller. Hence, the notorious "Winner's Curse"; whereby, when values are acknowledged as communal, the Prices paid by buyers, are inevitably "too high".

If it is theorised that throughout the economy Prices are arrived at via auction methods, then this is tantamount to an acceptance that monopolistic, or at the very least imperfect, power determines Price levels within that economy. The fairy tale we tell ourselves, of consumer sovereignty and negotiated price ratios, should be squarely acknowledged, as such, as a con-trick, of self-delusion.

Insight 134:
Subjectivism and Power

When value, and hence prices, are determined subjectively, distribution (and thereby allocation of scarce resources) is determined by arbitrary power in the form of money.

Indeed, scarcity is the application or manifestation of power. Without subjective valuation and associated distribution, power (in the form of wealth) could not be exercised by those with access to money.

Such subjectivism (in value) is a necessary condition for the exercise of wealth as the dominant expression of power. Economic power requires subjective valuation to be socially accepted, so that wealth emerges as the exclusive expression of power - wealth supplants physical might and other forms of power, as well as distribution based on need.

Wealth, or the access to money, effectively becomes the determinant of need, which itself is the exercise of monetary power.

Insight 135:
Emancipation from
Property Dependency

How can we reconcile Ellerman's notion and justification of the Democratic (Isocratic) firm, with its dependency upon property rights, to an incorporation of Process Philosophy within Economics?

The analysis of economic relations in terms of property would be compromised, if we question the very existence of entity formulated property.

Does commodification or concretisation of the abstraction of power promulgate and perpetrate into an entity, that which is only a transient process. The weather is such a similar transient process that cannot be transformed into ownable or vendible property - the weather cannot be owned, bought or sold.

In a similar way power is transient and cannot be commodified into vendible or transferable property. It is inalienable unto itself.

The *Capitalist Illusion* is that economic power is transferable. That it is possible to have power over power. Such power is not inherently inheritable, so deference to hierarchical procedures has to be inculcated and otherwise embedded into social norms. An apparently successful subterfuge.

Process Formulations
Processes may be formulated into various forms:

Transient Processes: (see previous above)

Permanent Predictable Processes: these are, as the nomenclature suggests, both permanent and predictable. They follow a discernible temporal path in terms of the events they generate.

Permanent Contingent Processes: these, although permanent temporally, are contingent upon other processes, and subsequent events, for the events they are responsible for.

Permanence in this context is not to imply that they are eternal, but rather they have the tendency to be continuously ongoing, within the prevalent state of affairs.

Contingency is effectively a continuum throughout this classification, when we consider transience an extreme form of contingency. When we view a process as transient, we are conceiving not necessarily its functioning, but rather its existence as contingent upon other processes' operations.

Even this differentiation could allow for demarcation in terms of the dependency and inter-dependency between processes.

Section 11
Business

Insight 136:
Profit and Business

Profits have long been recognized as in antagonistic competition with the reward to Labour.

In perfect competition, the rate of profit is zero. As such the purpose of business is to sabotage competition so as to create or enable profits. These profits exist as the negation of Labour's remuneration. The aims of business is to transfer wages (worker's earnings) into profits by sabotaging both the economy and competition.

Insight 137:
Notes on
The Problems with Business

Sabotage

Many, if not most, things (as vendible alienable property) are valued because they are scarce. But generally, things in this sense are not actually rare. They can be made with labour if we are willing to apply enough labour to the making of them. Thus, it is Labour, which is not a thing (i.e. not vendible alienable property), that is scarce and thereby valuable.

However, the purpose of business appears to be to make things and thus benefit from their value. Therefore, business needs to create the idea or appearance of scarcity in the property (things) it produces. As such, business will not be motivated to apply enough labour to make things sufficiently numerously to ensure they have no value. Business needs to *sabotage* production to ensure it can profit from its own self-induced scarcity.

For without scarcity there would be *perfect competition* and hence no profits. In a state of *perfect competition,* the whole product (the final surplus of production) would remunerate the workers, rather than provide profits to business.

The purpose of business is thus to sabotage labour in order to generate profits for those who do not labour. Capital is the power, or the processes of business, that converts the property of labour to the property of non-labourers.

Individualism

Business, as the pursuit of individual advantage may have been an instigator of social advancement, but it has always come with a cost. Society's evolution is such that it should eventually be able to free itself from those drawbacks inherent with business.

When J.S. Mill wrote that he believed the time was right for this transformation, those whose personal and financial interests lay with business sought the development of a new economics. As Karl Polanyi recognised, the major objective of this new economics was to transform the *Spirit of the Age* in favour of individualistic business somewhat in opposition to Mill's more social pathway of communal development. This Transformation[31] has been achieved via a methodological individualistic and subjectivist marginalism, otherwise under the umbrella term – Neoclassical Economics.

Some economists in the 19th century, such as Hodgskin and Ravenstone, recognized the conflict between business and Industry. Veblen coined the term *Sabotage* in the early 20th century to illustrate the disruptive effect of business upon productive output. In contemporary Political Economy, writers such as David Ellerman and Nitzan & Bichler are at the forefront of this position.

Whilst the term *Sabotage* is still apposite, the term Industry as the contrast to business is perhaps less so. If a new Industrial Revolution is to be pursued along the lines of Thomas Hodgskin, Thorstein Veblen and David Ellerman, it perhaps needs a new name for its main protagonist.

---

[31] As in Polanyi's book *The Great Transformation* (1944).

The current rise in political Populism could be interpreted as an outcry in favour of new relationships between people (as industrious workers) and the current establishment (as one dominated by business interests). The attractiveness of protectionist policies is a clamorous attempted reaction against business in favour of workers' apparent interests.

With the right economics and appropriate politics, it should be possible to stimulate a new *Spirit of our Age* that puts productive and social outputs before individualistic self-serving business interests.

In part this will require a new rationality that recognizes the overriding advantages of social action over the pursuit of short-term and short-sighted self-interest. Crucial to this will be the overturning of the Hobbesian myth - the *war of all against all*.

A *New* basis for Financial Relationships

Our present financial relationships are based on *money* being lent to people. Effectively people rent themselves in exchange for money. Would it be possible to have relationships based on money and capital being rented by people? Effectively a return to a system dominated by Trust (i.e. Money operating as an expression of Trust rather than an expression of Power). This would change the power relationship between those in control of capital and money with those having the need or requirement for the finance, although finance would then simply equate to Trust.

If our industrial relationships changed such that Capital could no longer rent (i.e. temporarily own) Labour, then the whole social nature of Capitalist relationships would essentially be changed. Such a change within employment relationships would necessarily have implications for the overall role of Capital in society.

At present finance is framed within power relationships that are parallel to those in employment arrangements. Effectively if we wish to charge the power asymmetry in the latter, it will also be necessary to do so in the former.

If we conceive a society where Labour hires Capital, then Capital becomes the tool of Labour; rather than Labour being the tool of Capital. Likewise, Capital must function as a tool of people in all aspects, not just in the employment sphere.

In financial terms payments for funds need to be (one off) fees for use rather than compounded interest payments. The problems of Capital's all engrossing power stems from its ability to command compounded interest. It therefore requires a curtailment or reversal of these arrangements to correct these problems.

Capital must be returned to being the servant of humanity, rather than being the Master of society.

Section 12
Policy

Insight 138:
Economic Policy

The only legitimate economic policy is to dismantle all existing economic policies so as to obliterate any impediments to the otherwise truly random results of economic activity.

Reality is inherently random. However, those who benefit from this randomness, will tend to enact policies so as to maintain their benefits, to the detriment of those less fortunate.

An inherited myth emerges and is supportive of this distortion of randomness. This myth is the denial of randomness. All outcomes cease to be random consequences, but the results of the extraordinary characteristics of those that are benefited.

Fairness ceases to be random and thus unbiased outcomes. Fairness becomes an inversed causality – those that benefit, must be better, for it would be unfair otherwise.

Cognitive dissonance will inevitably convince the rich that there must be a reason for their advantages.

Insight 139:
Buying British

The campaigns to "buy British" must be necessary as British goods tend to be more expensive than their foreign counterparts. If they were not, no campaign would be necessary (i.e. if they were cheaper). However, if we consume more expensive goods, we will be able to consume less goods, with our income.

Hence, a campaign to "buy British" will effectively impoverish the British people. Likewise, a campaign to ban or lower immigration, which amounts to an encouragement to only "buy British Labour" will effectively lower the real income of British consumers.

If foreign workers are not being employed, but replaced with more expensive British workers, then the price of their output will be raised. This means that the real wages in the UK will be lowered as nominal prices rise. Alternatively, if the price of output does not go up then the wages of the British workers will have to be cut - i.e. Real Wages will decrease. Either way British workers will be worse off.

Cheaper workers lower prices, which means more goods can be purchased from the same wages. This in turn equates to a rise in Real or relative wages.

Insight 140:
Theory, Policy and Practice

Economics is not a discipline such as medicine, where theory has a direct influence upon policies. Economic theory, at best, only influences or shades policy practices. Economic policy is subject to far more considerations than merely Economics.

Politics is the major determinant of Policy. Indeed, Politics is the discipline of Policy. Economic theory and considerations are just one of many alternative theoretical influences that feed into Policy.

The notion of Economic Policy is probably a misnomer, given its relatively minor position within the politician's hierarchy of concerns. For example, the steamrollering of austerity as a policy is repeatedly implemented for political ideological purposes, despite economic logic.

That being said, the vagaries and impenetrable convolutions of Economics and the uncertainty of the economy, facilitates its continuous use as an excuse for otherwise unpopular and difficult policies' enactment and justification. Economics is a good excuse for wayward Policy. A politician will always find an economist willing to back up their policy. Economists are often far too willing to play the politician's game.

Economic Schools at best suggest economic practices. The Pluralist should thus pick and mix these practices for expediency to meet ever changing practical purposes.

Economics should be an attempt to understand economic processes. Thereby, human experience, in the light of these processes, is itself a reactive process that formulates and progressively develops those processes. Economics should be the discipline that attempts to understand the inter-relationships of human social processes.

Insight 141:
Brexit

The referendum to leave the EU was akin to attempting to make a democratic decision as to whether we wanted "pigs to fly?". It may well be the majority's desire, but that democratic mandate has very little affect upon reality.

Other things, such as World Peace, hunger, and economic inequality may well be democratically desirable, but that will never be the necessary and sufficient condition to ensure their implementation.

The Brexit referendum was always politically illusory. Unfortunately, the relevant electorate apparently did not sufficiently understand this.

The idea that economic sovereignty could be clawed back from the EU to the British Government was an illusion. Economic sovereignty and power rest with capitalists and The Market. The EU, as a numerous and large entity, has more clout against the Market than a smaller entity, such as the UK.

The EU is likely to be more successful in its battle against business sabotage, than the smaller (weaker) UK. Even the EU may not be able to effectively counter business: the UK has very little, if any chance.

Sovereignty could be restored to the EU, but will not be to the UK.

Insight 142:
Tales of Ordinariness

Ordinary people often experience extraordinary circumstances. Those out of the ordinary situations being caused by the biases of unordinary people. Events are shaped by the ordinary simply because of the randomness of reality. The vast volume of ordinariness in the middle of the bell curve will tend to outnumber the comparatively lesser number at the bell curve's two extremes.

It is the ordinary that mostly saved us from the extremes and excessive biases of the few. Progress is the victory of the normal. Never have so many owed so much to so many.

There is thereby an inevitably in the disruptive behaviours of the abnormal few. However, there is likewise another inevitability in the harmonizing actions of the normal many.

Provenance, Benevolence and the Beneficent are the consequences of randomness, of the power of a normal distribution. The subjugation of biases, of the machinations of the abnormal few, tends to result in the "happy ever after".

Those who are so sure of themselves, that they attempt to shape the future, are inevitably foiled by failure. We could only shape and control the future if we knew what it would be. Its randomness, its unfathomability, is our defence. The vanity of the unordinary is fortuitously their downfall and undoing.

We may be inevitably blind to future history, but we can be secure in its progressivism.

The naturally conservative among us deny the Beneficent of progress and change, and thereby fear the future. They thus seek to conserve a status quo that they exalt as the best of all possible worlds and exhort the power of the few, the aristocracy of the unordinary, the out-layers of normality and the normal distribution. They thus attempt to inculcate fear into the vast mass of the normality of society.

Society, and its distributed beneficent, are the necessary consequence of a normal distribution (of all things) which is so loathed of the conservative, and perhaps explains their concentration rather on the individual and the denial of "society".

Insight 143:
Prophesy

A prophetic prediction is simply a statement of one of the numerous possible random outcomes. Prophesies all have a chance of becoming or of being true. Each as likely as any other. To be otherwise would be proof of bias. Bias against randomness.

We make choices out of the randomness of the events that befall us, in order to create our world.

The claim that any one outcome is a prophesy is an attempt to create a bias for that outcome. Prophesies are effectively biased to themselves.

Insight 144:
Law and Economics

The purpose of a law is to correct an Externality or other market failure.

All crimes amount to the perpetrator's enactment of an Externality. Such acts are the consequence of their failure to appropriately address such Externalities. Crimes are thus caused by the perpetrator's:

A]   Ignorance of the subsequent Externalities.

B]   insufficient or inaccurate valuation or miscalculation of the Externalities.

C]   Wilful disregard of the Externalities.

Laws are (or should be) the enforcement of socially acceptable standards and levels of Externalities.

Insight 145:
Command Economy

A Command Economy can be defined as an economy whereby what, and how much, to produced is determined by a particular agency rather by the market method of Supply and Demand.

It is generally conceived that the Government is usually as the only agency with enough power to enforce and maintain a Command Economy.

The Post-Keynesian position however is that Capitalists, as a tacit collective, have sufficient power to effectively enforce and maintain a Command Economy upon the rest of society.

_____

_____

Section 13
Miscellaneous

Insight 146:
Kant's Golden Rule and Utilitarianism

Utilitarianism can be seen as a reactionary response to the Enlightenment and more specifically Kant's imperative to treat people as ends in themselves, rather than means to an end.

Modern representative democracy can be understood as utilitarian, and as conceiving its voting population simple as the means to the end of the attainment of power. Modern business practices, similarly, can be seen as using its consumers as mean to profitably ends, i.e. Power.

What is it about Enlightenment principles, that engendered such an over-bearing response as Utilitarianism? For those in or with power the Kantian rule must be a very unsettling prospect. Their power is effectively the degree to which they can treat other people as means to their own ends.

It is in this mode that Thomas Hodgskin defined Capital as the power to control workers' Labour and thereby their legitimate products.

Business in this way, as both Hodgskin and Veblen emphasised, sabotages Industry. That sabotage amounts to capital's power to enable the few to treat the many as means to the own self-interested ends of profits and accumulation of more capital (i.e. Power).

If business was to continue sabotaging industry and the economy as a whole, the utilitarian creed was a necessary, if not fully sufficient, condition. Its further development with Pareto efficiency and Utilitarianism was an additional exploitative tool.

Is it possible or reasonable to attempt to formulate laws of human action in effect akin to Asimov's Three Laws of Robotics? This is the question we begin to investigate herein. These will intentionally also embrace the Kantian position, the imperative, to treat people as "ends" rather than "means".

Like Asimov's schema, these laws need to be hierarchical. They not only also need to be logical, but unquestionably acceptable effectively, to everybody.

At the top of the hierarchy, we should perhaps experiment by starting with Kant's Imperative: - Never act as if someone is a means to an end.

By using the term "act" it would also embrace the action of treating. From here we could look toward a law that is the default position when the first cannot be adhered to.

The controversy with this is that it goes against utilitarian principles and associated modern ideals of democracy. Indeed, if Kant's imperative is taken as the epitaph of the Enlightenment, then Utilitarianism can be seen as an oppositional proposition. The Utilitarian position can even be understood as a reaction against the Enlightenment and Kant's Golden Rule.

There is an off cited rule that "one should treat another as one would hope to be treated oneself". This tends not to get universal acceptance on the basis that it is based on a presumption that others have the same needs and desires as oneself. From a utilitarian perspective, this would be seen as irrelevant, as the onus is to treat people as necessary to maximise all possible utility.

Although, as Utilitarians tend to admit, utility cannot be measures or even effectively known.

Insight 147:
When Silvery Clouds Float
Through the Wildered Brain

Notes in response to
Enlightenment Now (2018)

Institutional Critique
On page 12 Steven Pinker argues that the Enlightenment sought progress through human institutions.

Whereas, the Perfectibility debate was concerned with progress via the Perfectibility of the Individual. The use of individuals' education and intelligence was to be used to perfect human institutions. Pinker's expression seems to be that human perfection comes from improvements to institutions, rather than the other way around.

Thus, for Pinker, Utilitarianism was a tool of Enlightenment judgement, used effectively as a rule of thumb, to judge and shape institutions and their instruments' (e.g. laws and rules) efficiency in promulgating individuals' Perfectibility.

Although Pinker previously mentioned Kant as a defining presentation of the Enlightenment, and specifically refers to the Kantian imperative (of people as ends not means), he appears to embrace the Utilitarian disregard of Kantian ethics, as Enlightenment.

Rather than conceive Utilitarianism as reaction against the Enlightenment, Pinker sees it as integral to the Enlightenment project. In this way it would appear that Pinker is unaware of Thomas Hodgskin.

Utilitarianism

When Adam Smith wrote his two most important works (*Theory of Moral Sentiments* and The *Wealth of Nations*) he did so a Moral Philosopher of the Enlightenment. His economics is not a Utilitarian creed. The Utilitarian Creed (as J.S. Mill clarified) was an ethical code, initially concerned with the equitable distribution of Utility. This well-meaning creed however was flawed and eventually floored by its apparent reliance upon that immeasurably Moral (i.e. mental) quantum - Utility.

Once cardinality had to be abandoned, it became acknowledged that Utility could only be quantified with ordinality. This evident weakness illuminated the issue of the incompatibility of qualifying individuals' idiosyncratic utility levels. Hence, Pareto efficiency and the perversion of the original various Utilitarianisms of Paley, Godwin and Bentham.

Equitable distribution of utility is now only acceptable as long as no one's utility can be diminished in order to improve another's. Thus, distribution can never be countenanced as a re-distribution.

In a Capitalist economy this means that any increase in societal wealth must be distributed throughout all society's classes. Any benefits that where allocated to a single class, would, proportionally, disadvantage the other classes.

If this logic is extended to individuals, it can be argued that if even a single individual increases their utility in absolute isolation, then everyone else would be Proportionately disadvantaged. This in turn highlights another fundamental issue, in that if utility is subjectively independent and idiosyncratic, then why would someone be disadvantaged by someone else's improved circumstances, or even affected.

If a person's mood changes so as to improve their utility level, that is more likely to subsequently improve other's wellbeing than diminish it. If an individual's utility is kept to themselves, it is unlikely to impact on any others.

If we accept the agnosticism of Pareto, there can be no assumed connection betwixt individuals' utility and thereby no prohibition on increasing or redistribution of utility. Indeed, it may well be that redistribution of some individuals' utility may increase rather than necessarily decrease the apparent utility of others.

For the anti-redistribution stance, using material wealth (or more simply money) as a proxy for utility is supposed to simplify such issues. Moneyed wealth is blatantly cardinal, even if the derived utility is not. It thus becomes Pareto Optimal to increase individuals' wealth if it can be achieved without diminishing another's money.

The presupposition is that a reduction in an individual's moneyed wealth cannot result their increased utility. The assumption requires strict adherence to methodological individualism and a presumption of non-satiation. It requires non-exchangeability of utility between goods. Which appears to make economic exchange Problematic. The agnosticism of Pareto morphs into nihilistic dismissiveness.

A New Enlightenment

A New Enlightenment would start with a shift away from the apparent nature of material things and event instances to a greater focus on the over-arching processes that generate, maintain, evolve and finalise those material and event expressions. Human attraction and attentions have long been to and on the mere instances of reality as the experience of our existence.

These moments of our being, and our attention to them, have been the basis of much of the progression of human understanding and development. However, an over concentration upon them can misdirect our efforts away from a more essential and fundamental comprehension of our condition and reality.

Without wishing to appear to be too derogatory much of our knowledge is superficial in that it is concerned with the surface appearances of nature rather than the underlying and underpinning principles that give rise to the apparition of reality.

The Individualism Paradox

Methodological Individualism is self-centred and exploitative; whereas Communal Action can be forgetful of the individual; in that Communal Action can treat individuals as expendable and as mere means to a greater social end.

There are competing logical arguments for Methodological Individualism and Communal Action that appear valid but are contradictory.

Methodological Individualism does not engage with the necessary social nature of human experience and existence. A truly individual person is necessarily less than fully human. An exclusively social being is likewise less than fully humane.

Perfect Competition may ensure certain human rights, but appears to deny many human (social) advantages. We need Perfect Competition consistent to and within a social context. Indeed, Perfect Competition without society would be contradictory, as it implies others in its competition.

Perhaps Perfect Competition is the necessary (and hopefully sufficient) condition to resolve both these individual and social paradoxes? Such a competitive solution would need to entail mutual inter-dependency without asymmetrical power relationships.

The problem with Perfect Competition is that the winners tend to gain asymmetrical power. Although the distribution of such power may be random, the outliers will necessarily disproportionately increase their power in relation to the others. Law and some other social conventions (e.g. interest), inevitably concentrate power in fewer hands.

How should society protect itself from asymmetric power without actually creating such asymmetries?

The elimination of compound interest and Monopolist power (and rent) may be indispensable measures.

An aspiration to increase societal wealth requires a commitment to a formulation of perfect competition that does not see economic activity as a zero-sum game. Rather a belief that economic activities are more productive when social, than when compared to individualistic principles and conditions.

Sums and Games

If economic reality can be conceived off as a game, then it relevant to consider whether it is a zero-sum game, or something more or less.

If it were a zero-sum game its players would be in a continuous struggle with everyone else to "win" their fair share of the spoils. There would also be an imperative to, at the very least, maintain the status quo, and one's lot therein. The maintenance of that status quo could be pursued in all good consciousness as not of necessity, depriving others of their fair share.

However, if we are in a negative-sum game, the struggle is more of a battle. We are faced with a fight just to survive and maintain bare subsistence. Others become distractors from our own continued persistence. Others can justifiably be considered and treated as means to our ends. Their struggling and even demise can be accepted as necessary to our own continuance.

In contrast to these bleak, one might dare say dismal visions, if we are able to enter a positive-sum game, then that would be a prospectus worth pursuit.

Within a positive-sum game, we are entering a world of surplus, where the continuous struggle to survive is abated. Others are no longer obstacles to our welfare or to be considered as tools or instruments for our personal betterment.

If one has confidence that we exist is a world of progress and human perfectibility, as the Enlightenment Philosophers did, then one is presuming the positive-sum game.

However, doubt casts its shadow across our horizon. The fear of negation of positive gains creates a guarded self-interest. Faced with relevant or even absolute disadvantage, securing what one has (conservation) becomes the order of the day.

Energy

Wealth is the control of energy. More practically, wealth is power over that control. When wealth can be created *ex nihilo* then everyone could be benefited, assuming we have and recognise a positive-sum game.

Production, as the human reaction against entropy, is the movement to more open, or expansive systems. The imperative to such larger systems, due to inherent difficulties in so doing, gives birth to a perceived need to maintain an exclusive control over that environment.

The openness of a system can be compromised by overuse, in terms of its limited resources and by the number of users taking advantage of its facilities.

Thus, not only is there a struggle to open up otherwise closed systems, but also to keep them relatively open. The finiteness of systems, and thus our exposure to entropy, is crucial to survival.

Humanity's dominance over our environment, as an ever-opening system secures our place as the dominant creature on our planet. That is until (if) we encounter a superior species in this regard.

War is a rather brutal and primitive attempt to be in this controlling position.

Scarcity

Scarcity exists only in the context of entropy. Particularly within a closed system (or economy). As social creatures, humans have the potential to counter entropy's negative effects and thereby reduce physical scarcity.

Life, due to entropy, is finite, making each person's time limited and thereby a scarce resource. Humanity, as long as its number or its knowledge increases, is not finite or subject to scarcity.

When the sun implodes, our major source of energy will disappear, making energy a scarce resource within our particular closed system.

Futures tend to depend on our ability to transcend the present limitations of our current closed system. Progress, in this perspective, can thus be equated to the continuous expansion of our otherwise confining environment - the opening up of otherwise closed systems - the breaking down of constraining barriers. Breaking the Cage.

In this manner much (all?) of human action could be understood as a process of breaking down our Cage (of existence).

- The alimentary imperative enables us to grow and provides the energy to live and act.

- The need to breed transcends us as individuals to an ongoing family or some other grouping.

- The need for reciprocal social acknowledgement transfers us out from our limited social environment. Fame and celebrity are likewise motivated.

This closed system Cage of the individual needs to be transcended both physically and intellectually. It is the acquisition and utilisation of knowledge that enables humanity to plot and execute its escapes.

As research is a process, it has no outputs. Publications can only ever be admissions of failures, whereby the researcher points out and explains their shortcomings and thus seeks assistance and guidance in resolving the problem or question.   Not for themselves, but just to add to the body of Knowledge.

Research
The process of research is the continuous improvement of that body of information, that perpetually incomplete quest for knowledge.   It will forever be incomplete as long as there are problems.

Not being burdened with the quest for Knowledge is the blessing of being freed from all problems. Unfortunately, death is the only condition we will have where we are no longer faced with problems. The only existence we have where we refuse to recognise our perpetual problematic condition, is one of a living death.

Education is concerned with revealing problems and getting people to recognise just what those problems are, to which we have yet to answer successfully. Education is highlighting what we do not know, within that base of what we think we do understand.

What we know is the background of solved problems that emphasises more of what we cannot resolve. The more we come to know, the greater revelation becomes clear on the nature of the problems we have yet to begin to find solutions for.

Educating is thus one of life's difficult problems. It is a continuous process not only for those we teach, but also for ourselves.   How can we teach when we have ourselves, so much to learn? Only by recognising and acknowledging our limits, as well as the process and problems of the continuously unfolding nature of problem discovery.

Enlightenment is a mutual and interdependent process of problem discovery and attempted resolutions. There are no finite solutions.

Humans act, as the apriorism of the Austrian School for Economics emphasises, because of their dissatisfaction and frustration with their current situation. Expressed another way; *Human Action* is our considered reaction to the complexities and problems we experience in the process of existence.

Alienation

To tell me to stop worrying is to alienate me from my humanity. To be human is to worry about problems. To smooth away problems and placate away worry, is to deny the essence of what it is to be human. Satisfaction erases the need for human action.

Insight 148:
Zeno's Paradoxes and Economics

The mathematical *Standard Solution* to Zeno's Paradox of "Achilles and the Tortoise" requires that there is assumed to be a logical numeric linear continuum

> The intuitive picture is that any interval or segment of the continuum is *a* continuum, and any continuum is a very special infinite set of points that are packed so closely together that there are no gaps. A continuum is perfectly smooth. This smoothness is reflected in there being a great many real numbers between any two real numbers. [32]

As such:

> Calculus ... can be thought of as a technique for treating a continuous change as being composed of an infinite number of infinitesimal changes. When calculus is applied to physical properties capable of change such as spatial location, ocean salinity or an electrical circuit's voltage, these properties are represented with continuous variables that have real numbers for their values. These values are specific real numbers, not ranges of real numbers and not just rational numbers. Achilles' location along the path to his goal is such a property.[33]

As such the use of calculus in economics is based on an assumption that all numbers in its purview are real

---

[32] http://www.iep.utm.edu/zeno-par/#H2
[33] http://www.iep.utm.edu/infinite/#continuum

numbers that themselves are infinitely divisible by real numbers. This may be mathematically so but is not economically so. For example, one economic agent cannot be divisible into any other number of viable agents – halving a human being does not create two halves as productive entities, but rather just a dead body.

Indeed, by this argument it seems that the use of calculus may be unsuitable for all human activity.

Calculus is the systemization of small changes – differential calculus. Human changes are not differentiable as human action is not smoothly linear but is irregular, unpredictable and not smooth. Human change is not infinitesimal, but are step changes; they are separate, non-continuous and discrete.

The change involved with inanimate objects may be smoothly infinitesimal, but once we are dealing with animate, especially sentient beings changes become distinct, disconnected, and detached.

Humans are incapable of making a choice pertinent to an infinitely (but continuous) small gradation. Their choices are often large and bold and often polemic to a binary or simply dualistic degree. Humans are thereby conceived of as making choices on infinitesimal matters that are literally inconsiderable and unsolvable to them – a considerable problem for both Methodological Individualism and Marginalism.

Differential calculus is necessary within a Marginalist formulation of economics, where all decisions are superficially made as marginal decisions, exclusively regarding infinitely small quantities of goods. However, decisions are not made, or even considered, on matters so infinitely small as to be otherwise generally conceived to be infinitesimally small as to be inconsequential.

Does this link to the idea that in marginalism, the rate of profit being made at the so called margin is effectively uneconomic, especially when compared to the average market rate of profit? Part of the question whether the maximum amount or rate of profit, or indeed utility, is sought in decision making situations.

Insight 149:
Notes on Sraffa

Sraffian profit distribution rates.

We need to be able to calculate a range of profit shares in a two commodity model where a surplus is produced in only one of those two commodities.

$$(X-Y) + (A-B) = (X + Z)$$

$$(Y) + (B) = (A)$$

Thus, if $Z = 0$

$$(X-Y) + (A-B) = X$$

$$(Y) + (B) = A$$

Insert "A" from this last equation into the previous:

$$(X-Y) + [(Y+B) - B] = X$$

If we are able to insert Z (as a rate of profit), into the latter pair of otherwise balanced equations, then we might be in a position of equating one of the commodities as Labour so as to determine wage as an equitable distribution.

Alternative approach to Sraffa's two commodity with surplus model.

The problem is with the nominal size of the surplus (in one commodity) we find it difficult to calculate the rate of profit. If we took the rate of profit as known (rather than the nominal size of the surplus), we should then be able to not only calculate the relate price, but also actual size of the physical surplus.

We will have just two unknowns (the quantities of the two commodities). The rate of profit will then of necessity give us a price as a ratio between those two commodities.

As such if we know the initial quantities of the two commodities and the rate of profit, we will know the relative price and the size of the surplus.

If these can be calculated, then surely, we should be able to change the unknowns such that rather than the size of surplus being the *unknown*, the rate of profit is the quantum to be derived.

This indeed may be how Sraffa himself resolved these issues - hopefully it wasn't this that took the majority of the forty-five year he spent writing his book.

Sraffa presented a simple (no surplus) two commodity model of product such that:

280 qr, wheat   + 12 t. iron   → 400 qr. Wheat

120 qr. Wheat   + 8 t. iron   → 20 t. iron.

(Sraffa, 1960, p.30

Let us simplify the nomenclature such that:

$$\left(\begin{array}{ll} 280\,X + 12\,Y & = 400\,X \\ 120\,X + 8\,Y & = 20\,Y \end{array} \right) \quad (1.)$$

In such a system the 12 units of Y used up in the production of X, have to be replaced with 120 units of X used up in the production of Y.

Thus, the necessary exchange ratio is 120X to 12Y.

This effectively equates to a price ratio of 10X per Y.

Rather than following immediate course taken in Sraffa's book, we will first investigate what happens with this system when there are productivity changes.

Let us, for example, explore what happens when the industry producing Y has a productivity gain such that it requires only 96X to maintain its output of 20Y (instead of the original 120. As such:

$$\left(\begin{array}{lll} 280X & + 12Y & = 400X \\ 96X & + 8Y & = 20Y \end{array} \right) \quad (2.)$$

Thereby, in such a system the 12 units of Y used up in the production of X, have to be replaced with 96 units of X used up in the production of Y.

Thus the necessary exchange ratio is 96X to 12Y.

This effectively equates to a price ratio of 8X per Y.

Therein the purchasing power of Y has decreased from 10 to 8 as a result of its increased productivity. Not only that, but the now surplus 24 units of X remain with the industry that last lagged behind technology-wise.

Further production enhancements would further exasperate the situation for the Y industry:

$$\left(\begin{array}{lll} 280X & + 12Y & = 400X \\ 90X & + 8Y & = 20Y \end{array} \right) \quad (3.)$$

Here the 12 units of Y used up in the production of X, have to be replaced with 90 units of X used up in the production of Y. Thus, the necessary exchange ratio is 90X to 12Y, which equates to a price ratio of 7.5X per Y.

The purchasing power of Y has further decreased as a result of its increased productivity. Not only that, but the now surplus 30 units of X remain within the industry that last lagged behind technology-wise.

One way for the Y industry to gain from its productivity improvement is to maintain the original price ration of 10:1 so the surplus (of 24 or 30X) is effectively transferred to the Y industry. This might be easier to achieve if its technological improvements remain unknown to the X industry.

This then (the advantage gained by undermining the necessarily arising Price ratio), may actually resolve into the motivation to technologically improve one's own production methods.

As a technological Price becomes evident, the resultant incentive emerges to use this exchange ratio so as to change what would otherwise be used within production (production goods) into surplus goods. These surplus goods subsequently being utilised either as consumption goods or further production goods.

From an Austrian Economist's perspective, goods of the Second Order are transformed such they can optionally be used as goods of the First Order or of Higher Order.

If we conceive that productivity is of necessity always improving, then equally necessarily, the Nature Price (as the technologically evident Price ratio) must always be emergent and diminishing.

Although as productivity improves throughout an economy, it should be acknowledged that the nominal Price ratio will be determined by the scale of the relative productivity changes. In a simple two commodity model if both industries productivities simultaneously improved at exactly the same rate then the Price ratio would remain unchanged.

A dynamic appropriately reactive Pricing system would apparently eliminate opportunities for surplus acquisition in this method.

What does this imply for a distribution regime that takes into account Ellerman's critique of Residual product distribution?

Example based on Sraffa (1960: p.7)

$$\begin{pmatrix} 280X + 12Y & = 575X \\ 120X + 8Y & = 20Y \end{pmatrix} \tag{4.}$$

In this set-up

- 12 units of Y traded at 15Y per X = 180X.

- The X industry needs 280 + 180X = 460X;

- their profit is 575 – 460 = 115.

- Their profit rate is 115/460 = 25%.

- Y industry inputs = 120X + 8Y = 120 + (8*15) = 120 + 120 = 240

- Y industry profit = ([20*15] - 240)/240 = (60/240) = 25%.

- It's 'fair' to each industry.

- Input ratio 460:240 = profit ratio 115:60

If we started with system (4.) without a surplus but applied an overall 25% profit, what effect would this have on our calculations?

Insight 150:
Sraffa's Price Determination with a Surplus

To solve Sraffa's Price determination for a two commodity system with a surplus one can address the problem in the following manner.

Initially let us simplify Sraffa's system such that:

$$A^x + B^y = E^x$$

$$C^x + D^y = F^y$$

In Sraffa's example he took iron as unity so the Prices (P) were expressed as a ration of wheat to iron. Hence is our system Y is unity and the price of X are expressed in units of Y. For the purpose of elucidating our solution we will drop the use of the X & Y superscripts. We are therefore trying to solve this system for an unknown P.

Our method is to assume that P is such that when applied to each line of these equations, the input to output ratios will equate.

As such:

$$[(A/P) + B] / (E/P) = [(C/P) + D] / F$$

Or alternatively as:

$$[(A/P) + B] \times F = [(C/P) + D] \times (E/P)$$

When P is thus found, this price can be used to determine the subsequent distribution of the surplus to the two industries and the system's rate of profit.

When this solution is applied to Sraffa's example in his Chapter II[34] the two ratios attained = 0.8 when (and only when) P = 15. This aligns with Sraffa's solution, and fulfils his criteria such that the exchange-ratio (or Price) "enables the advances to be replaced and profits to be distributed to both industries in proportion to their advances" (ibid).

Using this method we can draw up a table of the size of the wheat surpluses necessary to justify an increasing scale of prices from 10 through to 15, as below:

Price	Surplus	*Social* Profit
10	0	0%
11	36	5.8%
12	71	10.0%
13	106	16.1%
14	141	20.7%
15	175	25%

Three Commodities model with no surplus

$$aX + bY + cZ = dX \qquad (i)$$

$$eX + fY + gZ = hY \qquad (ii)$$

$$iX + jY + kZ = lZ \qquad (iii)$$

---

[34] *Production of Commodities by Mean of Commodities* (Sraffa, 1960, p.7)

Given circular exchange requirements

$$(d - a)X = bY + cZ \tag{iv}$$

$$(h - f)Y = eX + gZ \tag{v}$$

$$(l - k)Z = iX + jY \tag{vi}$$

By substituting (v) into (iv) for bY -

$$\therefore (d - a)X = (b \times e)/(h - f)X + (b \times g)/(h - f)Z + cZ \tag{vii}$$

Thus by rearranging X.s from lhs to rhs

$$[(d - a) - \{(b \times e)/(h - f)\}]X = [\{(b \times g)/(h - f)\} + c]Z \tag{viii}$$

Y can thereby be expressed in either X or Z by substituting the appropriate term from (viii) into (v)

$$(h - f)Y = e[\{(b \times g)/(h - f)\} + c]Z + gZ \tag{ix}$$

Insight 151:
Emergence

Life is emergent. Even the concept of this idea emerged [to me at around three o'clock on a September (12th) afternoon in 2014]. It cannot in reality be said to be my idea in a truly possessive property sense, but rather it is one that was the consequence not only of my thoughts, but also all that preceded them. The very nature of human existence, being social in essence is effectively emergent. One moment is the result of all it precedent.

A piece of art is valued, not only because of its creator, but also, perhaps even more so or even exclusively so, because of its perception and reception by others. What makes one piece stand out more than another is its necessarily subjective conceptualisation in the minds of others.

Social movements are not simply the sum of the participant actors, but are immeasurably greater than their constituents.

Knowledge is more than a simple collection of facts. A library is more than a mere collection of books.

A life is more than a series of singular events. Indeed, there are no isolated events.

Beauty is emergent in the eye of its beholders.

Insight 152:
Implications of
Constantly Falling Prices.

If Natural Prices, as the basis of Real Prices are always in a state of decrease such that goods are always becoming cheaper in real terms, this should be understood as having significant implications.

Money Implication

The Natural Price of Money could be conceived of as falling. As such the impetus for precautionary savings or holding of money is compromised. Money is held for precautionary purpose against the expectation that either prices of goods will increase (in relation to present earnings) or that the purchasing power of money in the future will decrease.

Price Implication

The price of goods in future will diminish in real terms. As such purchasing an amount of goods in the present greater than can immediately be consumed is a waste of resources. If goods are to be cheaper, then one only needs to buy "sufficient unto the day". This implies that labour needs only be expended in the here and now, as future labour, being necessarily more productive, will be remunerated at a greater rate. Why work an extra hour today, when an hour tomorrow will earn you more? Future labour being more productive will be able to acquire more goods than present labour.

Working today to earn more than is absolutely necessary to meet one's present desires, is effectively a waste of time, and thereby irrational.

However, this is predicated on the notion that the Natural Price decreases are passed onto those that labour. Given that we end up paying a Social Price, greater than the decreasing Natural Price, one needs to ask why this is? Such a question needs to be addressed by initially asking who benefits from such a regime, where labourers are not the beneficiaries?

The obvious answer is those that do not live on the results of their Labour, but rather unearned income. Rent and interest are the first two categories of unearned income, and once will conceive Capital as not being a productive agent (contrary to the Naïve Productivity Theory) then profit becomes the third category of unearned Income.

We need to include as actively productive agencies not only mental and physical Labour, but also the Labour of Superintendence, as well as entrepreneurial agency. We can thus tabulate this:

Earned Income	
Agency	**Reward**
Mental and Physical Labour	
Labour of Superintendence	Wages
Entrepreneurship	
Unearned Income	
Agency	**Reward**
Land	Rent
Capital	Profit
Money	Interest

John Bates Clark had a slightly different scheme whereby profit was solely the remuneration for Entrepreneurship such that Capital, together with Money were rewarded with Interest.

Earned Income	
Agency	**Reward**
Mental and Physical Labour	Wages
Labour of Superintendence	
Entrepreneurship	Profit
Unearned Income	
Agency	**Reward**
Land	Rent
Capital	Interest
Money	

Land, Capital, and Money are thus all forms of property that generate renumeration simply by their exclusive ownership. Labour, on the other hand, functions under a form of inclusive ownership.

Remuneration

Two things are remunerated, things (property) and activity. Only humans are active, whereas things, inanimate things, are inactive.

Remuneration is thereby allocated or awarded to activity or inactivity. These two forms should be entitled Labour and Interest respectively.

When Islamic economics forbids Interest, it is in this extensive form. In this way the bulk buying of things for subsequent individual sale at a "profit" is thus forbidden as interest, as is *Any excess paid or received on the principal.*

Why Social Price is greater than Natural Price.

Natural Price equates solely to the activity involve in producing goes. As such it is exclusively aligned with Wages. Social price is this Natural Price enhanced by:

a) The costs associated with inactivity, which we have above assigned as Interest.

b) The costs associated with the inflation of the money supply; Monetary Inflation.

Insight 153:
The Ethical Division of Economics

There is a clear bifurcation within Economics in terms of its ethical underpinnings. When Adam Smith wrote his Wealth of Nations it was the basis of Enlightenment Economics. As such, its ethical heart was aligned with Kant's Enlightenment Philosophy, and owed very little to what was to become the orthodox utilitarianism of the 19th century.

Whilst Kant's ethical code treated everyone as an end in their own right, utilitarianism conceived people just as means to overriding ends. The utility of society as a whole became deemed as more important than that of individual members of society.

Both schemes believed that individual actions would aggregate in such a way as he be socially beneficial, but utilitarianism, initially at least, saw utility as a quantifiable entity that could be numerically summed so as to maximise overall utility.

Eventually it became evident that Utility lacked numeric cardinality, although it could be considered with ordinality.

The Enlightenment's belief in the superiority of individual people also become the basis of the political creed of Classical Liberalism. This political liberalism was conjoined with economic utilitarianism with Pareto Optimality. This apparent solution became the illusion to placate liberal sensitivities and cardinality issues.

Thus, Pareto utilitarianism allowed the individual to exploit other individuals as means to their own end, if the alternative diminished in anyway the own ends.

When Werner Stack explored the origins of this split in his essay *The End of Classical Economics or Liberalism and Socialism at the Crossroads*, he noted:

In the first quarter of the nineteenth century there was still but one social ideal which men of good will strove to establish and secure: a society of liberty and equality as it had been conceived by John Locke and promulgated by Adam Smith. (Stark, 1943, p.51)

So when William Thompson (1824) argued that it was beneficial to social utility to tax a rich man to enrich two other poorer souls, he was reflecting what was to become the Utilitarianism of J.S. Mill (1863), who claimed that Utilitarianism was that creed which justified any action that added to social utility. If the gain of utility of the two beneficiaries of Thompson's redistributive tax was greater than that lost by the taxed individual, than such taxation was not only justifiable but a necessary action.

Insight 154:
Perceptions of Work

Work is often seen as a compromise between consumption and leisure. We have to work to be able to consume. Thus, to ensure that we continue to work, even though real prices are decreasing, we are encouraged to consume more. As a whole we all work more, which results in more consumables, which in turn results in our consuming more, which therefore necessitates in having to work more. This becomes expressed as "The Work Ethic".

Given the inevitable increase in productivity, then a steady decrease in work hours should be accomplished with increases in both population and living standards. This should be achievable as long as there are appropriate population and living standards, compensated by productivity gains.

However, greed, as formalised in the Economists' assumption of non-satiation, would undermine such a sustainable equilibrium.

Fear is the key to understanding why individuals act under this counter beneficial and thus destructive emotive motivation.

The communally rational "choice" would be to all work co-operatively (by way of a social compact) to reduce workloads, whilst still managing to increase output (through productivity gains).

However, a fear will be promulgated that some are gaining more than others, which is said to due to those gaining more being said to have cheated upon such a social compact.

Distribution, being affected by numerous random factors, will inevitably be uneven. Indeed, the assurance of randomness is the normal distribution curve. Any situation that majorly digresses from this normal distribution, should be recognised and acknowledged, as being influenced by some abnormalities, externalities or biases.

These artificial biases are what need to be addressed, both socially and individually, if we are ever going to reduce the workload humanity increasingly finds itself burdened with.

Insight 155:
Buy, Earn, or Purchase

There is an expression – "You can't buy these; you have to earn them". This is supposed to emphasise a distinction between merely buying something and having to work to earn that thing. Having the wherewithal to exchange money for something is not the same as having to work with effort and talent, to earn a reward.

An example would be a war medal such as the Italian Star or even a Victoria Cross awarded to a soldier for their service or gallantry. A Victoria Cross is known by the name of the person it was awarded to. So although Lord Ashcroft may be the owner of the largest collection of VC.s, over 160; he did not earn any of them. He just happens to have bought them.

In this manner, we can also say that those who were awarded the VC *paid* for it with their actions, indeed many *paid* for it with their lives. As such Lord Ashcroft did not pay for the medals, although he has legally bought them.

Buying is thus merely a legal act of acquiring legal (i.e. artificial) ownership, whereas payment is the original creative act that confers moral or *natural property* over an entity. That being said, legal ownership may be conjoined with moral property, but the former may be transferred, whereas the latter is inalienable.

The conceit of those that own something is their presumption, which they inevitably wish to enforce upon others, that it is also their moral property. Indeed, legal ownership is often used to enforce or even usurp moral property, at which point legal property, as possession of ownership, becomes the theft of moral property.

It is in this sense that Proudhon should be understood with his aphorism that "all property is theft". What should be comprehended is rather that all legalised property amounts to theft. Indeed, it might be seen that legalised property negates moral property even in those with an authentic claim to moral property.

Insight 156:
Incompleteness

Proposition 1: All mathematical systems are incomplete in that contradictory axioms and assumptions are necessary to describe any system accurately.

Proposition 2: Both humans and programmed algorithms (e.g. AI and mathematical) function with assumptions (rules of thumb), so as to be able to cope with the immense volume of information (and data) presented.

Consequent: The volume of data presented is a result of the concretisation of abstracts. As such, a process, rather than "thing" based, systematic analysis is far more likely to be able to resolve the incompleteness.

Questions: Would the application of process analytics be effectively little more than the use of quite specific rules of thumb?

If so, does process analysis provide the additional contradictory system of axioms and assumptions necessary to address the incompleteness dilemma?

Are we necessarily embracing Dialetheism?

Is Thingification simply another quite specific rule of thumb?[35]

---

[35] See George Shackle's *General Thought-Schemes and the Economist* (1964).

Insight 157:
The Right to Property

The right of property in a thing gives to the owner of that right the permission to occupy and utilise the thing in question. It is perhaps accurate to assert that when we own something, we have property of the right to occupy and use the object in question.

The right (or property rights) are what can be bought sold. It is only property rights that are vendible. These vendible rights can be transferred indefinitely (permanently sold) or for a finite period (rented or leased).

Some tangible things may be physically transferable when vended. Whereas other, such as land, cannot be physically relocated, given that they are themselves the location.

Whether intangibles can, might be a mute issue, when we consider that intangibles are effectively non-locational goods.

Indeed, if we conceive property simply as the right of use (and consider occupation as a form of use), then the whole matter of physical transfer and location is only a side-issue.

Thus, we may consider property merely as the right to use a thing (in a wide sense of *use*). Effectively property in or over a thing amounts to the power over a thing.

We are thereby left with four main questions to ponder:

i) What do we mean and encompass as "things"?

ii) Exactly what do we mean and encompass under the term "use"?

iii) To what degrees are all uses, things and rights inalienable?

iv) Can intellectual property be vendible?

Insight 158:
Agency and Agents

Economics tends to be concerned with agents and their agency. Such agency acts upon the constituent elements of the economy. These elements are usually simplistic expressed on the output side as goods and services, which are the resultant products of production. On the other hand, production's inputs are again simplistic expressed as Capital, Land, and Labour.[36]

Thereby, the agency of those within each of these classes are inevitably associated with their inputs to production. These agents tend to be categorised in terms of their associated inputs such that we have the three economic classes; Capitalists, Landlords and Labourers.

Not unconnected with this perspective, is the allocation of the resultant outputs in relation to those inputs. These remunerative outputs being profits, rents and wages. The Capitalist acquires society's profits allegedly in proportion to their input (capital). Likewise, the landlord and the Labourer receive their just deserts in their rent and wage. This system is apparently equitable as all agents gain their appropriate remuneration in proportion to their contributing inputs.

Thus, production is merely the allocating of outputs consequential to the various agents' input. Distribution (and to some degree) consumption of the outputs are the necessary, almost passive, outcomes of the relationships between the three classes of agents and

---

[36] Entrepreneurship may also be included as a factor of production.

their inevitable agency. With this schema, the agents are only affected by production in terms of their remuneration.

Capital may be used and replenished, but the Capitalist remains constant; as Capital, particularly when formulated as money (unlike the actual Capital goods), is not subject to depreciation.[37]

Land, as Ricardo originally specified, is the return "to the landlord for the use of the original and indestructible powers of the soil" (Ricardo, I, p.67). Thereby *Land* is not consumed in production.

Likewise, Labour is exhausted in the moment of production, but can be repeated and re-exerted in the next moment. Although the labourer may become fatigued, given appropriate time, they can be reinvigorated so as to repeat their work.

---

[37] This is an example of why money is considered by some as not a form of Capital, but is in contrast and even conflict with capital.

Insight 159:
Art

How can we transmit emotions?

Art can be understood as the communication of emotion, but is inevitability subjective and fallible.

Can there be an objective transmission of emotional feelings? Indeed, are such emotions quantifiable or measurable, i.e. objectifiable? To be transmitted, Art would have to be reified.

If emotions are understood as processes rather than things, can they be alienable? The concept of a process can be understood and communicated, but not actually transferred. It can be replicated or recreated, but not actually moved or relocated.

Bibliography

Adams, Brian, Frank, Mary Margaret and Perry, Tod (August 2008): *Mountain or Molehill? The Pervasiveness of Overstated Earnings Through the Expected Rate of Return on Defined Benefit Pension Plan Assets*
https://papers.ssrn.com/sol3/papers.cfm?abstract_id=1408215

Augusto Graziani's *The Monetary Theory of Production* (2003).

Bichler, Shimshon and Nitzan, Jonathan (2012): *Capital as power: Toward a new cosmology of capitalism, Real-World Economics Review,* issue no. 61, 26th Sept. 2012, page 77

Böhm-Bawerk, Eugen von (1884): *Capital and Interest: A Critical History of Economic Theory.* 1890 translation into English by William Smart.

Clark, John Bates (1883): *Recent Theories of Wages* Article iv in *The New Englander*, Volume xlii, May 1883. W.L. Kingsley, New Haven.

Clark, John Bates (1899): *Distribution of Wealth. A Theory of Wages, interest and Profits.* Elibron Classics Replica Edition of the 1908 Macmillan & Co, New York edition. Also Augustus E. Kelley (New York, 1965) reprint.

Darwin, Charles (1859): *Origin of Species.* 1951 reprint of 1872 sixth edition, Oxford University Print, London.

Day, Fred (2020): *Economic Insights Volume 1.* Praescientia Press

Ellerman, David (1990): *The Democratic Worker-Owned Firm.* Unwin Hyman, Boston.

Ellerman, David (1992): *Property and Contract in Economics: The Case for Economic Democracy.* Blackwell, Cambridge (Mass.)

Ellerman, David (1995): *Intellectual Trespassing as a Way of Life; Essays in Philosophy, Economics, and Mathematics.* Rowman and Littlefield, Lanham, Maryland.

Ellerman, David (2015): *On the Renting of Persons: The Neo-Abolitionist Case Against Today's Peculiar Institution*

Hall, Charles (1805): *The Effects of Civilization on the People.* Charles Hall, London; Augustus M. Kelley, (New York, 1965) reprint.

Haskel, Jonathan & Westlake, Stian (2017): *Capitalism Without Capital: The Rise of the Intangible Economy.* Princeton University Press.

Hetherington, Henry (1849): *Last Will and Testament* – reproduced in *From Cobbett to The Chartists*, edited by Max Morris (1948). Lawrence & Wishart, London.

Hicks, J.R. (1933): *Utility of Money*

Hodgskin, Thomas (1825): *Labour Defended against the Claims of Capital; or, the Unproductiveness of Capital Proved with reference to the Present Combinations amongst Journeymen.* Knight and Lacey, London.

Hodgskin, Thomas (1827): *Popular Political Economy: Four Lectures Delivered at the London Mechanics Institution.* Charles Tait, London.

Hodgskin, Thomas (1854): Review of *Knowledge is Power* by Charles Knight, *The Economist* (30th Dec. 1854, p.1454)

Hodgskin, Thomas (2019-20): *The Collected works of Thomas Hodgskin Vol.s I-VII.* Praescientia Press

Kellogg, Edward (1849): *Labour and other Capital; the Rights of each Secured and the Wrongs of both Eradicated.* Edward Kellogg, New York.

Locke, John (1862): *Some Considerations of the Consequence of lowering Interest and raising the Value of Money* (1692 edition):

Maitland, James (Lord Lauderdale), (1804): *An Inquiry into the Nature and Cause of Public Wealth.* Archibald Constable & Co., Edinburgh.

Marx, Karl (1963): *Theories of Surplus Value (volume iv of Capital: part. i).* Lawrence & Wishart, London.

McVickar, John (1825): *Outlines of Political Economy.* Wilder & Campbell, New York.

Mill, John Stuart (1859): *On Liberty.* John W. Parker & Sons, London.

Mill, John Stuart (1963-88): *Collected Works of John Stuart Mill*, Volumes i – xxix. University of Toronto, Press, Routledge, Toronto.

Mises, Ludwig Von (1912): *Theory of Money and Credit.* 1953 English translation, Yale University Press

Pienaar, M.D. (2014): *Intequisms: Accounting of Ideas.* Centurion, South Africa by Africahead.

Piero Sraffa (1960): *Production of Commodities by Means of Commodities.* Cambridge University Press.

Piketty, Thomas (2013): *Capital in the 21st Century.* 2014 Translation by Arthur Goldhammer, Harvard University Press, Cambridge, Massachusetts.

Pinker, Steven (2018): *Enlightenment Now : The Case for Reason, Science, Humanism, and Progress.* Penguin.

Polanyi, Karl (1944): *The Great Transformation: The Political and Economic Origins of Our Time.*

Proudhon, Pierre Joseph (1840): *What is Property.* 1966 English edition, Howard Fertig, New York.

Ravenstone, Piercy (1821): *A Few Doubts on the Subjects of Population and Political Economy.* John Andrews, London.

Ravenstone, Piercy (1824): *Thoughts on the Funding System and its Effects.* J. Andrews, London.

Raymond, Daniel (1823): *The Elements of Political Economy* (Volumes I & II). 2nd edition, F. Lucas, Jun. and E.J. Coale, Baltimore; Augustus M. Kelley, (New York, 1964) reprint.

Ricardo, David (1951-1973): *The Works and Correspondence of David Ricardo* Volumes i-xi. Edited by Piero Sraffa, Cambridge University Press, Cambridge.

Scrope, George Poulett (1831:; *The Political Economists.* Review of Malthus, Read and McCulloch for *The Quarterly Review* (Jan. 1831).

Scrope, George Poulett (1833): *Principles of Political Economy.* Longman, Rees, Ormes, Brown, Green, and Longman, London.

Seligman, Edwin R.A. (1903): *On Some Neglected British Economists.* Reprinted in *Essays in Economics* (1925), Macmillan and Co., New York.

Senior, Nassau (1836): *An Outline of the Science of Political Economy.* George Allen and Unwin reprint *(London, 1951)* of 1836 1st edition.

Senior, Nassau (1848): Review of J.S. Mill's *Principles* (1848) and *Essays on some Unsettled Questions of Political Economy* (1844) for the Edinburgh Review (1848).

Senior, Nassau (1854): *Political Economy a Mental Science*. Reprinted in *Selected Writings on Economics 1827-1852*, University Press of the Pacific, Honolulu.

Shackle, George (1964): General Thought-Schemes and the Economist: Woolwich Economic Lecture.

Shapiro, Ben (2011): *There's No Such Thing as "Crony Capitalism"* https://townhall.com/columnists/benshapiro/2011/09/07/theres-no-such-thing-as-crony-capitalism-n1175043

Smith, Adam (1759): *The Theory of Modern Sentiments.* Glasgow edition [1984], Liberty Fund, Indianapolis.

Smith, Adam (1776): *An Inquiry into the Nature and Causes of the Wealth of Nations.* Glasgow edition [1981], Liberty Fund, Indianapolis.

Stark, Werner (1943): The Ideal Foundations of Economic Thought. Kegan Paul, Trench, Trübner & Co., London.

Thompson, William (1824): *An Inquiry into the Principles of the Distribution of Wealth Most Conducive to Human Happiness.* Longman, Hurst, Rees, Orme, Brown, and Green, London.

Thompson, William (1827): *Labor Rewarded; The Claims of Labor and Capital Conciliated or How to Secure to Labor the Whole Products of its Exertions.* 1971 reprint, Burt Franklin, New York.

Torrens, Robert (1821): *An Essay on the Production of Wealth.* Longman, Hurst, Rees, Orme and Brown, London.

Whitehead, Alfred North (1929): *Process and Reality.*
1978 *Corrected* edition, The Free Press, New York

The BoE paper – "The Framework of Capital Requirements for UK Banks" (Dec. 2015)

BoE Consultation paper CS5/18). *The Bank of England's approach to amending financial services legislation under the European Union (Withdrawal) Act 2018*

Index of Insights

Index of Names

Names

www.ingramcontent.com/pod-product-compliance
Lightning Source LLC
Chambersburg PA
CBHW030617220526
45463CB00004B/1318